Fifth Edition

House Rabbit Handbook
How to Live with an Urban Rabbit
By Marinell Harriman

Drollery Press

To our daughter, Tania, and our rabbit Herman

Drollery Press, Alameda
Fifth edition 2013
Printed in the United States of America
9 8 7 6 5 4 3

Credits: All photographs by the author, unless otherwise noted
Design by Bob Harriman
Printing by CG Printing, Minnesota

Library of Congress Control Number: 2013930533
ISBN-13: 978-0-940920-18-7
ISBN-10: 0-940920-18-2

Drollery Press
2861 Barbers Point Road
Alameda, California 94501

Contents

Preface

Bed sharing: Herman and her friend Tania relax in 1982

RABBITS ARE COMPANION animals. When we open our doors to them, they can bring out some of our best human qualities: humor, sensitivity, and compassion. They can sympathetically soothe us when we are weary and capriciously make us rearrange our homes to suit their tastes.

As with the fourth edition of the *House Rabbit Handbook*, the fifth edition is no longer introducing the concept of "house rabbit" to a world unfamiliar with the term. That was the task of the first edition in 1985.

The fifth edition addresses rabbit caregivers of today, who supplement the information they read in a book with voluminous material they download from the Internet. Since keeping the information organized and accessible can be challenging, my goal is to provide basics in a nutshell and refer you to in-depth reading on particular subjects. The fifth edition outlines some widely accepted facts, how-to basics, and fresh discoveries.

No matter how thoroughly you read printed or electronic information, you will still need to learn by hands-on experience. Bunnies are excellent teachers, if you watch and listen. After thirty years of living with house rabbits, I am still learning new secrets from my current residents.

Certain truths have been firmly established among rabbit people: All rabbits are valuable as individuals, regardless of breed purity, temperament, or state of health. As the products of human interference rather than natural selection, domestic rabbits are human dependant and need human protection to survive. Domestic rabbits should live in human homes and enjoy the same level of care as other companion animals. They should be neutered/spayed and treated for illnesses by veterinarians. Rabbits are intelligent, sociable animals who require mental stimulation, exercise, environmental activity, and social interaction.

Sound familiar? It should, if you've visited www.rabbit.org. These truths were the building blocks upon which the nonprofit House Rabbit Society (HRS) was founded. Our first exposure to these truths took place by chance in 1981 in Alameda, California.

HERMAN'S WORK

My husband, Bob, and I had different plans in the early 1980s, which did not include a rabbit in our house. Those plans were laid waste by a black and white spotted rabbit, who hopped out from under the berry bushes in the far back corner of our yard. Herman, whose sex we misidentified, inserted herself into our lives and changed our regard for rabbits forever. She lived in our house, slept on our bed, and met us at the door when we came home from work. She taught us of the joy of having a rabbit in the house, and the hutch that Bob thought he would build in the backyard was never even started.

Her time with us was short, a little over two years. The veterinary medicine that we take for granted today was not available for rabbits then. When she became ill, we were helpless to save her.

I was devastated by the loss and unable to manage my grief, until Bob made the remark, "I don't want to forget about Herman. If we forget her, it will negate everything she ever meant to us."

The thought of diminishing her importance was as painful as the loss of her physical presence. No, I resolved, Herman will not be forgotten.

That began a two-year process of researching and interviewing that led to the first edition of the *House Rabbit Handbook*. Upon this course, I came to feel that Herman would work her way into our future as well as our past. She would bring about relationships with many bunnies to come. My "premonition" was later described in the *House Rabbit Journal*,[1] the print publication for national HRS.

During the next few years, Herman became a symbol. People from all over the world sent me photos of their bunnies, saying, "This was my Herman." They don't send me pictures anymore. Instead they post them on the web, which is even better. Herman's work continues.

Herman's place in house-rabbit history is that of a catalyst. She enlightened our perceptions of rabbits and disproved misconceptions. She caused caregivers everywhere to demand consideration, respect, and better quality of care for their rabbits. Without Herman, the *House Rabbit Handbook* would never would have been written.

In the course of telling Herman's story, we met animal rescuers and learned of the plight of discarded rabbits. That took us down a path that I still attribute to Herman's work.

ORGANIZED RESCUE

Rescuing surplus rabbits from local animal shelters in 1986 led us to the founding of House Rabbit Society in 1988. Seven of the people who had participated in the first edition of the *House Rabbit Handbook* formed the first board of direc-

tors of the new nonprofit corporation. In the next few years, other key volunteers stepped forward to shape its history and expand its reach to the international organization it is today. Events of the early years are described on HRS's website.[2] ■

1. Marinell Harriman, "Inside the Box," *House Rabbit Journal* IV, no. 9 (2003), http://rabbit.org/inside-the-box/

2. ———, "House Rabbit Society's 20th Anniversary," *House Rabbit Journal* V, no. 3 (2008) http://rabbit.org/2008-house-rabbit-societys-20th-anniversary/

Acknowledgements

IN PAST YEARS, I described the *House Rabbit Handbook* as the book that wrote itself. Due to the participants and supporters who contributed written and visual material, as well as editing and consultation time, my job as author was made easy. Since all useful information can't be packed into a single book with page and space limitations, many references are made to more comprehensive articles on the web and elsewhere. Specific sources are included in chapter footnotes, and additional suggested reading is listed on page 94.

Sidebar Authors

The following authors, who have extensive expertise in their subjects, have generously shared their knowledge and insight in their sidebars:

Margo DeMello, PhD
Carolynn Harvey, DVM
Susan Davis
Karen Johanson
Beth Woolbright

Mary Cotter, EdD
Susan Smith, PhD
George Flentke, PhD
Sandi Ackerman

Editors and Proofreaders

I would like to thank my special editors and proofreaders for time they have given to those tedious, behind-the-scenes tasks:

Beth Woolbright
Margo DeMello, PhD
Susan Smith, PhD

Karen Johanson
Terry Linscott

Photographers

Several of my favorite old photographs remain in the fifth edition, and some new ones have been added. Current and previous photographic contributions have been made by the following:

Jennifer Abernathy
Heidi Blais
Amy Bremers
Margo DeMello
Hugh Douglas
Ian Elwood
Amy Espie
Alison Geise
Joy Gioia
Bill Harriman
Bob Harriman
Tania Harriman
Kit Jagoda
Donna Jensen

Walter Jenson
Nancy LaRoche
Sandy Loey
Carolyn Long
Ken Mark
Stewart Martin
Christine Morrissey
Maureen O'Neil
Cassandra Parshall
Judith Pierce
Rich Seivers
Amy Spintman
Jim Stoneburner
Janis Wild

Care and Education

My gratitude continues to all bunny caregivers in shelters and veterinary hospitals and especially to the staff and volunteers at the Rabbit Center, HRS's international headquarters in Richmond, CA. As a model bunny-only shelter since 2000, the Rabbit Center also provides ongoing education.

The content of this edition has been influenced by the Master Seminar lectures held at the Rabbit Center in 2010. The speakers who gave presentations broadened our knowledge base on rabbit care. I highly recommend ordering the complete set of seminar lectures on DVD. See page 94 for the speaker list and ordering details. ∎

Chapter One

Characteristics

Learning to appreciate bunny "nature" will enable you to respond to your bunny's actions, reactions, positions, and postures.

ONLINE BROWSING can give you a fairly good idea of what rabbits are like. You can see a variety of photos and videos and read blogs by adoring bunny fans. You can observe the rabbits available in animal shelters. Moreover, many shelters and rescuers provide home-like settings, where you can see how bunnies might behave in a human house.

Even so, people who have recently adopted a bunny may be surprised that they have brought home an intelligent creature with an inquisitive mind that is constantly looking for activity.

The following pages describe some preferences, behavior, and general characteristics of house rabbits.

The Mental Makeup

RABBITS ARE COMPRISED OF PARADOXES that make them highly entertaining—inquisitive yet cautious, skittish yet confident, energetic yet lazy, timid yet bold.

They are crepuscular, meaning most active at dawn and twilight. They spend a long mid-day "down time," during which many will seek a quiet corner inside their pen or under a chair for a nap. This habit fits the schedule of working people who are away from home part of the day. Bunny may be just waking up when you arrive home and will be delighted to see what treats you bring.

Living low to the ground (floor, carpet), they are clumsy in high places. Yet, their explorations may take them from inside the closet, behind the sofa, or under the bed to the heights of dressers, desktops, and tables. A single youthful rabbit can lay waste to the contents of accessible shelves, delighting in pulp fiction and the daily news. And the clatter heard from the kitchen is most likely due to pots and pans being rearranged.

WITTY AND WILY

Rabbits solve problems, like pushing on doors that open outward and pulling with their teeth on doors that open inward. They learn to use a litter-box, to come when they're called, and to sit up and beg for a treat. They have a remarkable ability to remember furniture arrangements and where the snacks are kept.

They can learn procedures and routines at any age. Smart animals that they are, rabbits play games—with toys, with other animals, and with their humans. They play games of their own invention, punctuated by sudden vertical leaps and 180° turns in mid-air.

Consistent with those of other animals, rabbits' games mimic survival techniques. Just as predatory animals enjoy chase games, rabbits more often play getaway games. Sometimes carrying a prized possession (such as a cracker), one may run from imagined thieves. Or after yanking an envelope from a human hand, a frisky rabbit zigzags off with a "catch-me-if-you-can" dare to pursuers. And on many occasions, witnesses have observed rabbits playing follow-the-leader.

High-minded exploration: *Hopping with compulsive curiosity from bed to dresser, Herman stops to reflect.*

"Rabbits who live in our houses adapt to our schedules..."

FREEDOM TO PERFORM

Similar to other animals when allowed some freedom, rabbits perform beyond their supposed capacity. The key here is opportunity in a stimulating interactive environment. What individual expression can you expect from an animal who never gets out of a cage? A rabbit in a backyard hutch will be unable to do more than just sit there.

AGES AND STAGES

Like kittens and puppies, rabbits can be a handful when they are young. Most rabbits will mellow out at maturity. The stage of intense curiosity, hyperactivity, and frantic chewing and digging occurs at the height of adolescence (4–8 months) —a time that we recommend neutering or spaying. Bunny-proofing efforts should be heightened at this time, and plenty of litterboxes should be available in all bunny areas.

Some of the rabbits we rescued years ago were never adopted into new homes and have continued to live with us. As they settled in, they became easier to manage and very mellow. All are spayed or neutered. Our seniors (over eight years) move about a little slower and sleep a lot more and graciously accept friendship in their golden years.

EFFECTS OF SHARED OCCUPANCY

Rabbits who live in our houses adapt to our schedules and take up our habits. Like us, they are preoccupied with appearances and have fastidious grooming habits. They engage in household activities with other occupants. They learn many human words and can distinguish their names, as well as "Come," "Box," "Outside," "Yum," "Let's go," and a number of endearing terms and sentimental sweet-talk delivered in the right tone of voice. ■

Meticulous groomers:
Patrick washes his ears (above), while Daphne wipes her face (left)

Rabbitspeake

THOUGH RABBITS ARE CAPABLE of learning certain human words, it's more important for us to learn their language. By watching our bunnies from a close-up view, we can hear what they have to say when they are "speaking" to humans. In living with different people, rabbits may develop different "dialects," which are best understood by those who live with them and love them.

Just as in our own language, we have homonyms (the same word with different meanings) so do rabbits. The important thing to bear in mind is context. While a few rabbit "words" are communicated by nasal and vocal sounds, more often they are transmitted by actions or simple postures, which include whole-body smiles.

BASIC VOCABULARY

Peaceful stretch. Bunny flattens out in a smile on his belly with hind feet extended. When especially happy, toes may curl under or the feet may cross at the ankles.

Sideways flop. If you find your bunny flopped over on his side or back, it doesn't mean he has had a heart attack. The fluttering eyelids and whiskers indicate that bunny is contentedly in dreamland.

Presentation. Another smile in the horizontal position is assumed by the recipient of petting by a favorite human or grooming by another animal. All feet are tucked under, while the chin is laid out flat on the floor. This is how subordinate rabbits "present" themselves to their superiors. But a presentation is also used as voluntary submission to a loved one, meaning something like: Take me. I'm yours.

Crouching is a tense unrelaxed version of presenting, often with bulging eyes, when the rabbit is not enjoying attention, but rather frozen in fear.

Shuddering. This is a comical whole-body expression. If your hands emit an obnoxious odor—like too much perfume or carburetor cleaner—when you pet your bunny, he may try to shake it off. Sometimes after a rabbit is given medicine, he may shake his coat to rid himself of the bad taste.

Purring. This is a series of fast but light vibrations of the teeth and happily quivering whiskers—activated by gentle stroking behind the ears. It signifies contentment to the Nth degree.

Crunching is a second expression made by the teeth, when bunny is sick or feeling discomfort. Tooth crunching is usually a louder, slower grind, sometimes accompanied by protruding eyes.

Whimpering is a fretting little noise made by a pregnant or pseudo-pregnant female, who is plead-

Phoebe's foot phonetics (above) stand for happiness, friendship, comfort, and a general sense of well-being. Lapin laughter (below) is manifested in Chessie's joyful wake-up yawn.

ing not to be disturbed. Some rabbits whimper when you try to pick them up or move them.

Wheezing sniffs combine vocalizations with nasal sounds to "voice" a protest.

Clucking. A pleasant sound is the faint clucking made by a bunny who has been given a particularly tasty snack. It always means, Yum, yum!

Licking/grooming. This is obvious affection. Rabbits lick each other and sometimes human friends.

Nudging/huddling. More ways to show affection involve sitting close. These friendly gestures are often overlooked by humans. Instead of licking, many house rabbits nuzzle nose-to-nose with their human friends. Nudging your ankle or tugging on your pantleg means, Notice me.

Honking/oinking. Because rabbits draw very little distinction between sexual and social behavior, many expressions are identical. Neutered males and spayed females may still court—circling each other (or your feet). Soft honking or oinking is a love song, also used to solicit food and attention. A honk can mean: I want you, or maybe a treat.

The body tells it:
Using her clearest language tools—rigid posture, ears pulled back, erect tail—Phoebe speaks her mind when she is caught stealing cat food.

Photograph: Tania Harriman

"You might be warned of "danger" that the furniture has been rearranged."

The chin tells it: *A wicker hamper (upper left) is desirable property for Daphne to claim.*
The ears tell it: *Bunnies posing for adoption photos (upper middle and right) explain where their attention is engaged by the direction of their ears.*

Chinning, a benignly assertive gesture, is a peculiar way of claiming property. By rubbing their under-chin scent glands on the items (undetectable to us), they mark them as possessions.

Nipping. This is not necessarily an angry remark. Rabbits are often saying, "Move over." Sometimes it means, "I'm scared. Put me down!"

Snorting/growling. In anger this may be just a warning or it may coincide with a grunt-lunge-bite directed at an adversary. This kind of anger is predictable and can be prevented.

Erect tail. The excitement shown by a tall erect tail can be caused by the threat of an adversary, the proximity of a potential lover, anticipation of tasty treats, or simply the appearance of a new toy.

Tail twitching. In a competitive or a courting context, rabbits may twitch their tails from side to side and spray their conquests. A modified assertion is simply tail-twitching as a form of "back talk."

Ear assertions. Ears send and receive messages. Alert forward ears say, I hear you. Alert bi-directional ears say, I hear you and something else, too. Menacing, tightly pulled-back ears say, Watch out!

Kicking. In protest, kicking is high and to the back. In play or combat, rabbits kick to the side.

Dancing. You'll know it when you see this frolicking series of sideways kicks and mid-air leaps accompanied by a few head shakes and body gyrations. Many rabbits have literally danced their way into human hearts.

Thumping. This has several meanings: I detect something out of the ordinary, or I have an announcement to make.

Rabbits thump over many things—sights, sounds, smells, and things that we don't sense. It might be a danger signal, and then again it might not be. You might be warned of "danger" that the furniture has been rearranged.

Yet, this sense of propriety is the very thing that can make a rabbit a highly suitable individual to share your home. ∎

The feet tell it: *With a back kick in anticipation (below), Cumin shows her delight before entering her outdoor playground.*

When Bunnies Use Biting Words

MOST BUNNIES will never bite a human, and those who do are often the most capable of loving relationships. If you understand why bunnies bite, you can avoid being bitten.

Testing. It's common for baby rabbits to go through a period of testing their teeth. If your bunny decides to test his teeth on you, I advise a small screech. This is a sound rabbits make in dire distress. He will understand that this is serious.

Move over. Rabbits may nip whatever is in their way. It can be another rabbit who is blocking the water bottle or a human arm that is confining a rabbit to a lap. Screeching may work, but better yet, avoid using part of your body as a barricade.

Zealous grooming. When grooming each other, rabbits pull out burrs and chew foreign particles entangled in each other's fur. Keep this in mind when your rabbit friend is licking your sleeve or pant leg and comes to a seam or wrinkle that could be interpreted as foreign.

Defense. Objects coming from below eye level may appear threatening. Don't stick your hand up to a rabbit's nose to be sniffed as you would to a dog or scratch under the chin as you would a cat. Also, your extremities, hands or feet, may be judged separately from the rest of yourself, so don't assume that your bunny doesn't like you if he distrusts your hands. It may take him a while to perceive those foreign objects as part of you.

Side approach. A human hand is all the more threatening to a shy rabbit when it is reaching in through a small side-opening cage door. As you invade her "safe" haven, she backs into the far corner. You must find a way to approach from the top, even if it means installing a new top-opening door

or enlarging the one on the side. Or consider discarding the cage altogether in favor of a pen.

Aromatic fingers. If you have been eating pretzels or dicing carrots, don't stick your fingers immediately into bunny's chomping area.

Possessiveness. Unspayed females (or unneutered males) may be particularly protective with their possessions, and it's best to clean the cage or pen when it is unoccupied.

Misdirection. A human referee may incur a misdirected bite for trying to intervene between two rabbit adversaries—in much the same way that a person gets scratched by grabbing a cat from an attacking dog. A bite-attack may also be triggered by the scent of a "foreign" rabbit on your clothing.

HABITUAL BITERS

My most affectionate rabbits of today were once labeled biters. Their gradual but thorough transformations are described in the online archives of the *House Rabbit Journal*.[1,2,3]

Also on House Rabbit Society's website, there is a comprehensive FAQ on aggression in rabbits.[4] If you have a "biter," please read these articles.

Our rule has always been to meet animosity with benevolence and avoid situations that provoke an attack. Converting a biter is a rewarding experience—one of my favorite story topics. ∎

1. Marinell Harriman, "Who Wants a Mean Rabbit," *House Rabbit Journal* II, no. 2 (1990) http://rabbit.org/who-wants-a-mean-rabbit/
2. ———, "To Love a Mean Rabbit," *House Rabbit Journal* IV, no. 1 (1999), http://rabbit.org/to-love-a-mean-rabbit/
3. ———, "Socializing the Antisocial Rabbit," *House Rabbit Journal* V, no. 8 (2011), http://rabbit.org/socializing-the-antisocial-rabbit/
4. Susan Davis, "FAQ: Aggression in Rabbits." HRS website, http://rabbit.org/faq-aggression/

Chapter Two

Adoption

Commitment is needed for a period of ten years or more.
Advance preparation helps make that commitment.

HUMAN ATTITUDE is a greater factor than rabbit behavior in determining the success of the adoption. Instead of insisting that your new housemate meet all of your needs, concentrate on learning about and meeting your bunny's needs.

This chapter will list basic facts to consider before adopting your first rabbit, as well as new considerations for previous adopters.

If you have an unplanned rabbit, such as a rescue from the street, and you are trying to avoid surrendering her to an overcrowded shelter, it's not too late to learn. You can foster her until you find her a suitable home, or you can educate yourself in rabbit care and keep her. After evaluating your own situation, you may find that you are an ideal bunny adopter.

Choosing a Rabbit

Incoming rabbit (above, top) is befriended during his quarantine period by Beth Woolbright at HRS's Rabbit Center.
Adoption Counseling: Anne Martin (second from top) gives adopter Sindy Carlson take-home tips on bunny care.
Bonding pen (right) provides a place for Kirby (white bunny) to get acquainted with Princess at the Rabbit Center, while his humans, Kelli Jimenez and Matt Davis, supervise the introduction.

WHILE YOU CONSIDER what you want in a rabbit, consider also what you have to offer in yourself. Would your new bunny choose you? Take the following self quiz to find out.

Furniture arrangements: Am I willing to make some compromises?

Vacuuming: Am I willing to vacuum a little more hair than I would in a rabbit-less home?

Bunny proofing: Will I take necessary safety measures to protect my bunny and my house?

Sense of humor: Do I have it?

Social time: Will plenty of social interactivity be available in my home?

Supervision: Will I supervise the activities of other animals or children around the bunny?

Relocation: Will I take my bunny with me when/if I change my residence?

Veterinary care: Will I take my bunny to the vet when he is sick or injured?

Education: Will I learn "rabbitspeake"?

SELECTION PROCESS

Your search for a rabbit usually begins with visits to animal-adoption websites, followed by a visit to the physical locations. You may be attracted to a certain type of aesthetic appearance, but it's highly advisable to pay attention to the personality descriptions listed by the adoption counselors, who have been trained in evaluating dispositions and matching them with compatible families. For instance, a meek and timid bunny might do fine with one or two individuals in a quiet home. A feisty, inquisitive bunny may be better able to tolerate the noise and activity level of a home with multiple family members of various ages.

It's best that you don't have too many preconceived notions as to breed, size, and age. No matter how gorgeous the bunny might be, it's more important that your personalities and the lifestyles are harmonious. Think first of the home you are providing and who would be happy there.

COMPANIONSHIP

If your house sits empty house all day, consider adopting a bonded pair. Two rabbits are no more bother than one, and they would keep each other company while you are away. Animal shelters and HRS foster-volunteers are delighted to place already neutered and bonded pairs in good adoptive homes.

Photograph: second on left, Ian Elwood

If you are adopting a single rabbit into a household with other animals, think about the kind of companionship your other animals can offer. Read chapter 4 to plan your careful, safe introduction.

A BUNNY FOR A BUNNY

Special considerations do need to be made in selecting a friend for another rabbit. Personality may be important here, but not size. Age is an issue only in meeting differing exercise needs in "May-December" matches. Since second adoptions are welcome at most shelters, the staff will often help with the matchmaking.

If a bonding pen is available and all rabbits are neutered/spayed, adopters can bring in their first rabbit to choose his or her own companion. This process is detailed by Beth Woolbright on page 50. The visiting rabbit may choose a different partner from what his humans had expected, but they usually defer to their bunny's choice.

ADOPTING FROM A SHELTER

Bonding service is one of the many advantages you get when you adopt from an animal shelter or rescue group. You can get an already spayed or neutered rabbit, sometimes micro-chipped, and one who has perhaps already been socialized by volunteers. When you adopt from a shelter you are directly or indirectly saving a life.

The adoptable-rabbit cage, vacated by the bunny you bring home, is filled by one who might have been headed to euthanasia. That bunny will now have a chance at finding a home.

If you are not yet sure of your willingness or readiness to commit to an adoption, you might try volunteering at your local animal shelter where you can learn about bunnies first hand. Volunteers

Young volunteer (above), *Alivia Abernathy, socializes bunnies for New Mexico HRS. Her job is to figure out which bunnies do well with kids. By pretending to ignore Sarah rabbit, Alivia allows Sarah to make the first social gesture.*

Foster program: *adoptable bunnies (left), who are fostered in private homes, spend time at HRS's Rabbit Center in Richmond, CA. The additional exposure increases their prospects for adoption.*

often bring in hay, vegetables, and toys and help socialize the bunnies. Shelters with a volunteer presence are able to bunnies get out of the cage to exercise in pens several times a week. Volunteering would provide you with an opportunity to get acquainted with different bunnies and even socialize them prior to bringing a bunny home. ∎

Photograph: top, Jennifer Abernathy

Bunnies with Young Humans

Quest on the floor: *Rabbit Vic (above) pursues the possibility of cookie crumbs on his toddler friend, Rian Harriman.* **Mesmerized** *by a gentle hand (below), Cocoa bunny gazes lovingly at her human companions, five-year-old Aoife Blais and ten-year old Aemilia Blais (who is doing the petting).*

Before you adopt a bunny into a home with children under seven, consider how much time you have for working with both rabbits and children—or postpone the bunny adoption until the children are older.

A NEW BUNNY IN A HOME WITH CHILDREN

If you are convinced that you can manage both, start looking at larger rabbits. Parents often think they want a small bunny whom their children can pick up. A far better choice is a rabbit with some heft that the kids cannot pick up. Parents don't expect children to pick up the family dog. Why should they pick up the family rabbit?

Your preparations should include extending your education in child-bunny matters, especially safety, for both. A most comprehensive, in-depth FAQ has been prepared by House Rabbit Society, that includes a set of rules based on the ages of the children. Anybody who has children or will have

children with their rabbits should read this extremely useful material.[1]

A NEW HUMAN BABY IN BUNNY'S HOME

Adoption counselors encourage parents to wait until their youngest child is at least seven before adopting a rabbit. But if you already have a bunny in your house and you are starting your human family, the last thing we want you to do is dispose of your rabbit. Many conscientious parents have successfully expanded their families with animals and small humans. My own grandchildren grew up with pre-existing rabbits in their home. Expert advice on keeping rabbits when starting a human family comes from parents themselves.[2,3]

WHEN TOGETHERNESS IS A POSITIVE THING

For all its challenges, having children grow up with rabbits can be advantageous for bunnies, as well as their small humans. Why not enlist the kids in services they naturally perform well? Children, who are compulsively touchy-feely with their loved ones, may be the first to find abnormalities. My own daughter pointed out lumps and bumps on our rabbits that needed to be checked.

When young volunteers showed up at my foster home, I decided to have them write down what they saw while sitting with the bunnies in their runs. To my surprise, they made remarkable observations of the bunnies' behavior and what they might be feeling. What a marvelous

1. Carolyn Mixon, "FAQ: Rabbits and Children." HRS website, http://rabbit.org/faq-children-and-rabbits/
2. Susan Davis, "Rabbits and Children: Safety and Happiness in a Shared World," *House Rabbit Journal* IV, no. 9 (2003) http://rabbit.org/rabbits-and-children/
3. Bill and Amy Harriman, "Bringing Baby Home, *House Rabbit Journal* II, no 7,http://rabbit.org/bringing-baby-home/

Photographs: upper, Bill Harriman; lower, Heidi Blais

way for a child to develop observational skills!

Whatever the mix of dispositions and ages in the human family, a responsible adult must be the primary caregiver, not only for the rabbit's safety but also to set an example. When parents are seen solving problems with more bunny proofing and additional litterboxes rather than discarding the rabbit, they are teaching a most valuable lesson in commitment. In doing so, parents are preparing their children for some of the best things in life. ■

Sharing snacks and moments of contentment (above), three-year-old Will Douglas indulges eager Dorothy with the treats she deserves.

Learning Kindness From Animals

BY MARGO DEMELLO, PHD

NUMEROUS STUDIES have shown that there is a link between the abuse of animals and violence towards humans; that children who engage in animal cruelty are more likely to commit violent acts as adults.

But scientists and animal advocates are now finding that the corollary may be true as well: that children raised in an environment in which animals are loved and nurtured may grow up to be nurturing, compassionate adults.

The research on this subject is not yet conclusive, but we do know that parents play a major role in the development of humane attitudes in children by exposing them to pets and teaching them, by example, loving care. We also know that there is a positive correlation between having pets as a child and developing a concern about the welfare of other animals.

But does this necessarily translate into a concern for humans as well? Since the Victorian era, parents have been bringing home pets to teach kindness to children, in the understanding that children who bond with animals will develop empathy towards humans, and new research is beginning to confirm this. What is most intriguing about this new research is that the type of animal one lives with, and the level of bond one forms, may play a large part in this.

No one has studied the relationship between children (or adults) and their rabbits, or how it may correlate to how rabbit caretakers feel about others, but from knowing hundreds of rabbit lovers, I can make a couple of guesses.

First, I think that living with a house rabbit definitely teaches us kindness towards other animals. Countless rabbit people have changed how they eat, how they dress, and what products they buy because of the relationship they've formed with their rabbits, who are, after all, farm and laboratory animals, as well as pets. It seems that for many rabbit caretakers, their love for their rabbits is globalized to include other animals as well. But do we take our love and extend it to humanity as well?

There's no way to know for sure, but certainly the hundreds of House Rabbit Society volunteers use their love of rabbits to not just help rabbits, but to help people as well, forming connections that are deep, meaningful, and worldwide. That just may mean something. ■

Margo DeMello, PhD, *is co-author of* STORIES RABBITS TELL *and* WHY ANIMALS MATTER. *She is president of HRS and teaches sociology in Albuquerque, NM.*

Big Bunnies, Big Hearts

BY SUSAN DAVIS

*A **big appetite** keeps big Bruno receptive to carrot gifts from his human, Phoebe Brand*

WE WEREN'T PLANNING on getting a third rabbit the day we met Bruno. In fact, my two children and I felt quite blessed with our existing menagerie: two rabbits, two mice, and two fish. But when we walked into the House Rabbit Society Rabbit Center one sunny afternoon and saw Bruno lolling contentedly in his cage, our hearts did a little flip flop.

It might have been the huge ears that turned gracefully in our direction as we greeted him. It might have been the giant back feet—feet that easily dwarfed our existing rabbits' back feet put to-gether. Or perhaps it was his kind, curious expression as he gazed at the kids. It was a look that seemed to say, "Well you're awfully short for humans. Do you know how to pat?" Whatever it was, my then five-year-old daughter looked up at me eagerly and said, "Can we get him, Mom? Can we?"

It's a question that parents hear from their children all the time, and it's one that I have learned to respond to carefully. Children are a lot of work. Pets are a lot of work. I love having children and pets, but I'm deeply committed to keeping my collec-tion of both at a sustainable level. Moreover, our young mini-Rex, Spotty, had never bonded with Maybelline, our other, rather sen-ior, rabbit. If we were to get a third bunny, we'd have to be ab-solutely sure that he'd enjoy our lively family, including Maybelline. I could handle three rabbits, but only if at least two of them got along.

So I looked at my daughter and gave the classic Mommy re-sponse: "Maybe."

One advantage of getting a rabbit from the House Rabbit Society is that the guardians know the rabbits personally. After ask-ing the shelter staff about Bruno's temperament, we lifted the giant bunny from his cage and put him in a pen with the children. He promptly stretched out between them and fell asleep with his chin on my daughter's shin. The matter was settled. A few weeks later, after shelter staff helped us bond Bruno and Maybelline, we brought him home.

Lots of people who come to our house are a little nervous about Bruno. Big bunnies just look scarier than small bunnies. But although Bruno on his hind legs is as tall as my four-year-old son, he is by far the gentlest, calmest rabbit I've ever met, espe-cially around children. We have learned from all of our rabbits that different animals have differ-ent personalities and needs—that a rabbit like Spotty craves peace and quiet, even if a rabbit like Bruno enjoys the kids. That's a crucial life lesson for all children and one of the main reasons I raise my children with animals. ∎

Susan Davis *is a freelance writer and co-author of* STORIES RABBITS TELL. *She and her family live in Alameda, CA.*

Handling

*We handle our rabbits in ways to make them comfortable with
human touch, allowing us to give them better care.*

HANDLING IS THE FIRST STEP in socializing our rabbits. For rabbits in shelters, socializing betters their chances of adoption. Timid rabbits become friendlier to humans, and aggressive rabbits become more trusting and less defensive.

Handling our rabbits includes touching, petting, and lifting—all prerequisites to providing them with essential grooming and medical care. The goal is being able to do it safely.

Rather than wait for an urgent situation in which you must grab your rabbit and run off to the vet, get your bunny accustomed first to handling on less stressful terms. Spend some time just being nice.

Building trust: *Ways to get started*

***Quiet repose:** Rhea bunny basks in the affection of her favorite human, Lily Martin.*

RABBITS ARE NATURALLY SOCIABLE. They interact with toys, with each other, and with other animals. To encourage interaction with you, keep her close to human activity and included in your daily life. If you are away at work all day, make proximity a priority when you are home.

Predictable human behavior helps your bunny feel safe. How else does she know what to expect? She will see how nicely she fits into your routine when you are passing out the veggies.

STEPPING UP GRADUALLY

Your bunny may not come to you already socialized and ready to accept your intimacy. Petting is one thing. Holding her captive on your lap is another. Lifting and carrying her is still another. You want your bunny to be comfortable with all, but it may require patience, especially if you are dealing with a shy or aloof rabbit. You will need to work up gradually to lift-and-transport mode.

Starting with play may be your ticket in. Toss her a ball. If she nudges it and bumps it back, you can start a game of "catch." Some bunnies also enjoy a chase-the-towel game with their human playmates. Drag a towel around in a circle and see if she takes the bait. Playing together is a form of communication that may well establish the groundwork for more intimate interaction.

IN YOUR FACE

The most direct way to establish intimacy with a rabbit is to take the same communication path that the rabbit does—nose-to-nose. Many rabbits are more trusting of your face than any other part of your body.

Some of my disabled rabbits respond much better to my constant prodding and messing with them after I have their habitat raised to a height where I can easily offer face contact with them.

KEEP TALKING

Although rabbits do not often vocalize, they are happy to listen to a friendly human voice. Talk to, at, and around your new bunny and have lengthy phone conversations with friends.

I discovered this bunny fact many years ago. Five newly arrived rabbits from the shelter waited in cages next to my phone, while I scheduled neuter and spay appointments. Continuing on to other conversations, I spent most of the afternoon on the phone. About two hours into the afternoon, I glanced around to find every one of the rabbits stretched out or rolled over in complete relaxation.

BE AN OBJECT

Rabbits choose to sit close to each other. To cozy up with you, let bunny initiate it. Occupy the same space and then read a book (see page 17). The bunny will come to you because it's in her nature to investigate you as she does the other objects in her environment. There is no need to grab, hold, restrain, or coax her into your lap. She will get there eventually on her own.

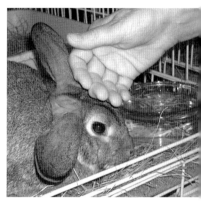

When making your lap available to a bunny, protect yourself with adequate clothing or a towel spread across your legs. You will be glad it's between you and her toenails. Don't blame your bunny for trying to get a secure foothold.

GRADUALLY GRADUATE TO HANDS

While your rabbit is first learning who you are, your hands may be visually frightening. You must make it clear that your approaching hand is not a threat but a giver of rewards. And as Nancy LaRoche advises, "Never lie to your rabbit."[1]

When the back of your hand is greeting a new rabbit for the first time, approach directly from the top of the head, not under the chin, and don't offer your fingers to sniff (see "Defense," page 14). Make sure she accepts strokes on her head and back before attempting the lower parts of her face. Rabbits groom each other around the eyes, top of the nose, top of the head, ears, and down the back. Stroking them in these areas feels friendly.

PETTING FOR THERAPY

After many years of using our companions to soothe ourselves, we are now learning that we can give back in kind. Techniques for stroking, massaging, and touching animals are used increasingly in their therapy. Ways of improving our petting skills have been excerpted from Karen Johanson's web article[2] into her sidebar on the following page. ■

Lap preparation: A towel is spread (upper left) across Amy Harriman's lap before Lilac hops on.
Toenail grip: *Don Wild of San Francisco (lower left) pays a deeply felt price for unprotected flesh.*
Back hand: *A new bunny (upper right) may find the back of your hand to be less threatening.*
Invitation to bite: *A chin-level approach to a bunny (lower right) is putting your fingers at risk.*

1. Nancy LaRoche, "A Glimpse into the Emotional Life of a Rabbit." Master Seminar 2 (2010). DVD: See page 94
2. Karen Johanson, "The Power of Petting," *House Rabbit Journal* IV, no. 10 (2004)http://rabbit.org/the-power-of-petting/

The Power of Petting

BY KAREN JOHANSON

TOUCH IS ONE of the primary ways we communicate our love for our animal companions, and we have the power to calm, relax, and even heal through this physical contact. With a little knowledge and desire, we can improve our bunnies' quality of life by simply fine-tuning our petting.

Start by greeting the rabbit and letting him know that you're there to give him love. Understand that the big person entering his home might appear very scary, and soothe him with a quiet voice and soft demeanor. Let him know that he's safe and that you'll return him to his spot soon.

Get him resting quietly in your lap, and start your massage by running your fingers gently along his whole body, using light, firm strokes and searching for bumps, hollows, heat, cold, tension, or sensitivity. If you find a troubled area, you can repeat your soft movements over the spot or simply rest your hand there for a moment. Chances are that the warmth, energy, and love you transmit will help soothe it. While you pet him, be sure to watch your bunny and note how he reacts. Pay attention to what areas he likes touched most and least, then be sure to always start his massages at the good spots before working on troubled areas. For example, gently rub his ears a few times, then continue your stroke over a sensitive location. Quickly return to the safe spot for a few more loves, then stroke the "danger zone" again. By keeping your bunny relaxed and concentrating on the positive feelings, you can slowly attune him to being touched elsewhere without taking fright. However, remember that fears don't dissipate in one day, and it will take some time before he lets down his guard; and if you're nervous, take deep breaths and exhale slowly. Let him know that it's safe.

Like us, rabbits can hold lots of stress in their necks and shoulders, and stroking these areas may help release anxiety, fear, and even grief. Use your thumb and index finger to massage small circles over his cheeks, at the base of his neck, and over his shoulder blades. Then gently run your pinkie a few times down his spine between the shoulder blades. Stroke the ears from base to tip with long, gentle pulls or massage along the top of his feet between the bones. If he relaxes and starts purring after a few minutes, you will know you've found an area he likes.

Whether you have a nervous little friend or a rambunctious troublemaker, your companion will appreciate the attention you give him and hopefully respond to your ministrations so that you and he can live a healthier and happier life together. He will recognize your increased sensitivity to his world and reciprocate with greater trust and affection. The knowledge that you may be increasing his quality of life is just a bonus. So pet with intent, and enjoy this time you have together.   ■

Karen Johanson *volunteers at Tri-Valley Humane Society and is also a medical assistant to Dr. Carolynn Harvey at the Rabbit Center in Richmond, CA.*

Lifting: *Without high anxiety*

WE LIFT OUR RABBITS WHENEVER it is necessary—to remove them from danger, to medicate them, or to perform certain cleaning and grooming tasks. Their skeletons are fragile, however, and it's important to lift and handle them properly to avoid broken bones.

You will probably discover that your bunny doesn't particularly like to be picked up and carried. All rabbits are a joy to watch, but not all are a joy to pick up. Your bunny may enjoy cozying up beside you, but being lifted and carried is a different matter. But since there are times when you *must* pick up your rabbit, it's best to prepare in advance for this inevitable action.

For this reason I recommend a daily exercise in lifting and handling by just picking her up and setting her down again. A brief, non-stressful lift followed by a small reward will help a rabbit overcome the fear of being lifted. Our formerly reluctant Phoebe caught on quickly. She soon began to circle my feet, tripping me, if I forgot her treat when I set her down.

Two positions that I use are shoulder-rump and feet-to-chest. I lift all large rabbits by the shoulders and rump simultaneously.

BIG BUNNY LIFT

To pick up a large rabbit from the floor, walk up confidently, get behind her, put one hand under the chest and one under the rump, and lift—with authority. Don't act timid. My technique is to hold the hindquarters firm and low to prevent kicking. My veterinarian does it just the opposite, with the bunny rolled into a ball. Either way, the feet are kept from getting into a kicking position.

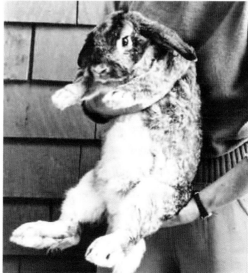

Large bunnies seem more relaxed when they can see where they are. The hand on the chest can be fairly loose. I keep a firm hold on the hindquarters, even grasping the tail if the bunny seems squirmy.

Photographs: left, Bob Harriman; right, Amy Espie

"Lifting your bunny becomes easier as she becomes familiar with the process."

From a floor position (upper left), lift a small bunny towards you. The feet can begin to curl upward as they come closer to your body for support. *From a cage* with a small front/side door (upper right), you need to support the bunny's front end as soon as possible, while scooping the back end towards you.

Heart-to-heart (above), shown by Anne Martin, is the holding preference for small bunnies, who are already facing you.

Caution must be used in setting bunny back down. This is a time that they often leap in anticipation. If you feel your bunny kicking right out of your arms, drop into an immediate squat on the floor. Reducing the height will reduce the chances of injury to your bunny or yourself.

SMALL BUNNY LIFT

Smaller rabbits are usually better picked up from the front. Place one hand under the forelegs and one hand under the rump and bring her towards your body. She will be less apprehensive as you bring her closer. Curl her hind feet upward until they're resting on your rib cage and her front feet are resting on your collar bone. Small bunnies feel most secure when braced against your body.

This lifting method makes an easy transition to the comfortable heart-to-heart holding position. It also is best for children (over eight) who are able to use their whole body for support of the bunny.

UP AND OUT

Rabbits can be lifted from a top-opening cage or pen the same way as from the floor. Top-opening doors are much easier for you than front or side-opening doors. The hardest lifting situation that you can possibly encounter is pulling a rabbit, of any size, through a small side-opening door. To get bunny out, reach in and place your hands on top of her head, stroke her from head to tail, and then scoop her toward you. The trick is to get your body close enough for her to get a footing with her front paws on your collar bone. This will make her secure enough to be pulled out the rest of the way.

Lifting your bunny becomes easier as she becomes familiar with the process. Talk soothingly at the same time you lift. Remember that she is being asked to go from a position of her choosing to a new location of your choosing. Reward her when the task is done. ∎

Photographs: far left, Ian Elwood; upper left, Bob Harriman; upper right, Amy Espie

Chapter Four

Space 4

Your arrangement of space should allow for a harmonious integration of your bunny's lifestyle with yours.

BECAUSE RABBITS have a strong sense of territory, most of them prefer to "own" some real estate. Even a bunny who has free run of your entire house wants a secure place for a home base.

Your bunny's area should be close to where you spend time, so that you can have some interaction. It should also have plenty of natural light and shade from direct sunlight. Bunnies' most comfortable temperature is 60°–75°, but more cold than heat can be tolerated.

Space arrangements are shown on the next few pages.

Living Space: *How to set it up*

Shared space: *Rosey and Kirby hang out on top of the chest of drawers in Carolyn Long's study in Glendale, WI.*

Free-running rabbits do not necessarily have unrestricted access to the entire house. There may be one or several rooms that are off limits, depending on how much bunny proofing you have done. This is not a denial of freedom. Bunnies often limit themselves. For many years I had free-running rabbits in the living room. There was no fence to keep them there, but they had no desire to go anyplace else. That was home.

Shared rooms: The most popular shared rooms for rabbits and their humans are dining rooms, studies, family rooms, and living rooms. A bedroom can be good place to share; but if you have extra shy bunnies, they may hang out under the bed, and you will never see them. If you want to socialize with them frequently, you might think of a more interactive room. On the other hand, bold and boisterous bunnies may enjoy bouncing around on top of your bed.

Dedicated rooms: If you want to set up a dedicated bunny room, make sure that the occupants have companions and that it's near human activity. Use a baby gate or see-through fencing. Don't have a solid closed door between you and your bunnies.

CAGES: WHEN AND HOW TO USE THEM

A cage is not a home in itself. It can, however, be part of a more extensive housing plan. With a door opening into a large pen with ramps, tunnels, and exercise equipment, the cage becomes simply a place to go for quiet time.

To provide comfortable resting space, the cage should be three–four times the (stretched-out) adult body-length. Remember this if you now have a baby bunny in a starter cage.

Two-story condos, connected by a ramp or a step-up, can add space within the same footprint. However, all cages and condos should be thought of only as bunny bedrooms, not as their entire play space. A condo can be expanded easily by attaching a pen to it that adds play space.

Use a small cage only if you have open-door policy. That is, keep it in a large bunny-safe area

Photograph: Carolyn Long

"The smaller the cage, the more time was needed outside it."

with the door always open so that the bunny truly chooses when to be in it. The cage should have large front/side-opening doors. If it includes a top door, be certain that it clamps securely from the outside, so that it can't be pushed up from inside the cage (posing a risk of strangulation).

Although we try to allow our bunnies all the freedom possible, cages should be closed when used as sick beds for ill or injured bunnies. I have a cage set-up in my bunny room, where I can confine a bunny with a back injury or keep a hypothermic bunny warm. It's also easy to drape a sheet over it and use it with a vaporizer.

In the past, we were asked how much un-caged time should the bunny have. The rule was that the smaller the cage, the more time was needed outside it. While we still may differentiate between resting space and running space, the two are now more often merged, with the use of adjacent exercise pens and larger spaces. ∎

Two-story condo *(above) opens to a larger bunny space in Alison Geise's home in Encinitas, CA.*
Living-room set-up *(left) includes an open cage, lots of hay boxes, and places to lounge in Margo DeMello's house in Placitas, NM.*

Photographs: above, Margo DeMello; upper right, Alison Geise

Pens: *The modern housing preference*

A LARGE WELL-FURNISHED PEN can be the housing solution in itself. Although you can construct a pen from scratch, store-bought pens are inexpensive, easy to use, and can be adapted to fit in nearly any home.

Wire shelving panels come in 14-inch squares that clip together in modules. I use these and like the flexibility of being able to reshape the living spaces, building them up or out, to fit the number and nature of the bunnies who live here. For instance, my older rabbits no longer need high fences, so a single panel is sufficient in height. I keep the upper decks covered with a rug or board to prevent feet from slipping through wide-mesh wire.

Metal-wire exercise pens (or x-pens), sold in pet supply stores, are by far the most popular rabbit housing of recent years. They can be expanded by adding sections and can be arranged in a variety of shapes. They are available in several heights.

Wire shelving panels (above), clipped together, form a pen, which sits on a FRP-covered plywood platform.
***Exercise pen** (right) is exquisitely furnished for Ozzie and Izzy with basics plus enrichments.*

Plastic lattice "play yards" (for human toddlers) are available in department/variety stores. They can also be expanded by adding sections. Some rabbits chew the plastic; most do not.

All pens can be folded down, moved about, or stored. A pen is a good investment when you begin your life with bunnies. Panels clipped together can also be used as fencing to divide space creatively.

FLOOR COVERING

Even bunnies with the best litterbox habits might spill hay and debris all over the floor. If the bunny area is on vinyl flooring, tile, or concrete, sweeping may not be a consideration. If it's on carpeting, however, you might consider setting the pen on top of a patch of linoleum or a chair mat. Or you can lay down a small paint tarp or even a bed sheet, to catch debris.

In our own bunny room, we use the same durable floor surface as the HRS Rabbit Center habitats. FRP (fiberglass-reinforced plastic) is glued onto plywood. The slightly bumpy surface gives bunnies a little traction but is highly cleanable, virtually chew proof, and available at most home-improvement stores.

FURNISHINGS

Well-furnished rabbit areas contain a variety of fixtures and supplies. Some are strictly utilitarian, while others are intended to be used for comfort and recreational purposes.

Water bottle. Hanging water bottles with sipper tubes take up

less space than crocks and make better use of small areas. Keep bottles out of direct sunlight (which encourages the growth of algae). Bottles should be checked daily, changed weekly, and washed with soap monthly. Check the sipper tubes daily for clogging.

Heavy clay crocks keep water fairly cool but occupy some floor space. Water in an open bowl is easily contaminated and should be changed daily.

Food dishes. Pellet bowls are made of clay, plastic, or stainless steel. Heavy clay crocks (smaller versions of water crocks) are less likely to be tipped over. If you want to use designer pottery, be sure that it is lead free. If you serve bunny salad on a platter, it's best to use unbreakable plastic.

Hay hanger. If you're not putting hay in a litterbox, a nicely stuffed basket can be used for bunny's hay supply (caution on attached toys, page 39).

Washable rug. If your bunny runs on hard surfaces, give his feet a rest with padded areas. Soft fake-fleece rugs are ideal, as well as indoor/outdoor felt carpeting, cut to machine-washable sizes.

Towels/baby blankets. These are useful for padding a cage shelf, or rolled up as pillows around the edge of a pen, or as wicking material underneath a soiled rug. Any fabric with large holes or raveled, stringy edges should be removed.

Litterbox(es). Various sizes and shapes are available to fit your bunny's space. They come in designer colors to fit your decor. Buy several. Some even have a lowered entrance for special needs.

Toys, large and small. As you will see in the next chapter, activities stimulated by toys are necessary for many reasons. All bunny spaces should be furnished with a wide selection of playthings. ∎

Lattice play yard (above) is usually shaped into a hexagon or an octagon. This one shows Peggy Sue with her furnishings.
Extended bunny space (left) accommodates toys with a large footprint. Scooter climbs over a tunnel while Baxter sits inside it.

Bunny Proofing Your Space

ANY PART OF YOUR HOUSE that is exposed to a bunny resident should have protection in place. Move valuable books, magazines, and potted plants out of grazing range. All electrical cords should be enclosed in vinyl tubing or moved out of reach. Rabbits cannot resist nibbling on these long "vines."

COVER-UPS

Anything that hides or encloses a forbidden article, we call a cover-up. Numerous items would adequately serve this purpose, but you will want to find some that blend in with your home decor. Here are some not too obtrusive solutions:

Chair mats can be purchased at office-supply stores in a variety of sizes. They cover problem areas of linoleum, hardwood flooring, or carpeting.

Seagrass rugs serve the same purpose as chair mats but are intended to be chewed and replaced.

Protected area: Oliver inspects the world from a safe place (above). *Seagrass matting* protects the couch from Peggy Sue's teeth and toenails (right). It gets rolled up when guests want to sit there.

Wooden bumpers are thin strips of untreated wood (furring strips), tacked onto a baseboard to protect the baseboard and serve as a chew block.

Plexiglas in 24-inch sheets can protect wall areas above baseboards without being too obvious.

Vinyl tubing is sold by the foot in hardware stores, and it comes in a variety of diameters. With a sharp utility knife, cut the tube lengthwise and push the electrical cord inside.

Furniture arrangement. This is also a way to hide wiring. Block the access to the electrical outlets with a piece of furniture.

Blanket throws can protect against toenails and teeth when tossed across upholstery or beds. In some situations you can use seagrass as a "throw."

REPELLENTS

The use of repellents has diminished over the years in favor of more pleasant alternatives, such as chew toys. Repellents are any of those odors or tastes that bunny finds repulsive. Pet repellents for cats and dogs sometimes work for rabbits. Check for safety of any product that you spray on the furniture. Is it safe to inhale or chew?

PREVENTION BY DIVERSION

You can take preventive measures to hide forbidden items or make them undesirable, but the most rewarding prevention is the addition of activity and recreation. This is done through exercise, toys, and a stimulating environment. Equipment used for achieving these ends are shown in the following pages. ■

Chapter Five

Play Activity 5

Destructive behavior, such as chewing or digging into your carpet, can be diverted into healthy projects for your rabbit.

PLAY SPACE AND PLAYTHINGS are important extensions of your bunny's basic necessities of food and water and a place to sleep. We cannot expect our rabbits to lose their natural urges to chew, dig, explore, and claim territory when they move into our house. But we can provide outlets for these needs with safe running areas and an abundance of toys to channel their energy in a desirable way.

By including these provisions, we are giving our rabbits "power to make choices in their daily lives and setting up their environment so they can successfully choose appropriate behaviors."[1]

1. Susan Brown, "Empowering People and Animals through the Science of Behavior,"
   http://behaviorconnection.com/About_Me.html

Photograph: Margo DeMello

Exercise: *Setting up playgrounds*

RUNNING AREAS might be included in the living space if the space is large. The type of activity performed is influenced by the shape of the area—long, wide, high, low. Exercise areas can be expanded vertically by adding ramps or step-ups to multiple levels. This allows climbing and jumping, but horizontal running space is also needed. Most exercise needs can be met inside your house with either a large around-the-clock living space or access to additional rooms for playtime. Going into a different play area often stimulates more activity. If your bunny remains in the same area, you can rotate stimulating toys.

Opportunity to exercise should be provided at least four hours a day or thirty hours a week. Not all rabbits take advantage of their opportunities, though, and you may need to provide encouragement in the way of equipment (page 36).

A long hall at the Rabbit Center (above) entices Roselyn to run the length. *Passages* to predator-proof play areas (upper right) are provided at River's Wish Animal Sanctuary. *X-pens with lids* occupy the backyard (below), where Donna Jensen often sits with her bunnies.

OUTDOOR PENS

A covered outdoor playpen might serve for daytime exercise, as well as an enclosed porch or balcony that's attached to your house. "Enclosed" means full fencing on all sides and overhead, even at upper-story levels. Predatory birds can and do snatch rabbits from balconies. Also, do not leave a rabbit unattended anyplace with public access, such as your front porch.

Portable pens. People who like some outdoor time for themselves can set up an x-pen (same kind as we use indoors) within a fenced yard. As you sit and read or do nearby yard work, you are there to fend off any hawks, cats, or any other predatory animals. The floorless pens can be rotated around the yard so that the bunnies have fresh grass to chew. Make sure the grass is pesticide free and not frequented by nocturnal wild animals (with possibly contaminated feces).

If you can't stand guard every minute, then the pens will need tops. Walter Jensen constructed the ones shown on the left by snapping together pvc piping into a frame and stretching heavy netting over the frame. Cable ties secure the tops to the pens, using two tops for each pen.

Photographs: lower left, Walter Jensen; upper right, Kit Jagoda,

Stationary runs in my own backyard now sit on a slab of bricks, which are hosed off occasionally. The eight-foot-long wood frames are heavy enough to stay in place. Step-through gates at the front and hinged wire-mesh tops give us walk-in access. In wet weather, we lay clear corrugated-plastic panels (patio roofing) across the tops of the runs.

At the beginning of the latest warm season, we "fly proofed" the runs with fiberglass window screening (sold in rolls at the hardware store). It was very easy to staple screen skirts around all sides and tops. We were quite pleased with the results—no flies or mosquitoes.

Dogs can't get into our fenced yard, and neighborhood cats can't get into the runs, so the runs can be unattended for short periods during the day. They are unsafe for night use, however, since we have raccoons in our area.

Before your bunny goes outside, take extra care to know your area and prepare for potential predators in your neighborhood.

Many other solutions are discussed in the *Journal* archives[2] and Seminar DVDs,[3] which tell you how sanctuaries and foster homes in various regions have created safe exercise runs that are predator proofed for their areas. ∎

*A **covered run** (above) is furnished with a rug at one end, a pile of hay and a cardboard tunnel at the other, and a plastic playhouse in between.* ***Mandatory exercise*** *(left) is included in the bunny procession to and from their pens.*

2. Beth Woolbright, "Great Outdoor Exercise Set-ups," *House Rabbit Journal* V, no. 1 (2006)
   http://rabbit.org/great-outdoor-exercise-set-ups/
3. Kathleen Jagoda, "Predator Proofing to Keep Rabbits Safe." Master Seminar 2 (2010). DVD: see page 94

Playthings: *How bunnies use them*

G YMNASTIC TOYS—those that entice climbing on, leaping over, running through, diving into, or sliding down—keep bunnies physically fit. Smaller toys—those that spring, swing, bounce, roll, or make noise—keep rabbits mentally engaged.

Chew toys of any size should be of untreated, non-toxic material. Natural wicker items, such as those made from cane, rattan, willow, reed, and bamboo are good choices. Rabbits need plenty of indigestible organic fiber, but not the synthetic fiber in your carpet or sofa.

Nudge-and-roll toys are propelled by bunny's nose, but sometimes they are tossed or chewed instead, They include large plastic balls or woven willow balls, empty soup cans or salt cartons, paper-towel spools, and toilet-paper spools. When you stuff a spool with hay, it becomes a chew toy rather than a roll toy, and it will soon disappear. Even though stuffed spools need to be replaced frequently, you have an ongoing source of spools.

Climbing toys for human toddlers can entice your bunny to climb and leap.

Ramps can be used for bunnies to get where they want to go—and exercise on the way.

Tunnels: Wicker tunnels are available in pet supply stores. Cardboard concrete forms, sold in building supply stores, also make good tunnels. Packed with paper, they can be digging projects.

Towels on a slick floor provide something for bunny to scoot around, bunch up, spread out, pat then roll up and scoot around again.

Hay tub: This is more than a litterbox topped with hay, so make it deep enough to dive into and

Large ball *with cutouts (above) offers Ashe a choice of rolling or tossing.* **Cardboard maze** *(below) offers exploration from every angle.* **Plastic tunnel/slide** *(lower right) provides climbing opportunity.*

Photographs: upper left, Judith Pierce; lower left, Margo DeMello

dig around. The exercise is not in eating hay but jumping in and out of a deep tub or box.

Baskets/boxes: large ones in a stack attract bunnies to climb and explore. Small ones are good for chewing. Wicker baskets come in many sizes and shapes. Bunnies love them all. You can find them at pet-supply shops or at www.busybunny.com.

Loose straw is for chewing exercise rather than nutrition. Offer it in a bale, a bag, or a large box.

Organic-fiber rugs include sea-grass rug squares, rice mats, and bamboo mats, which can be chewed if pesticide free (check supplier sources).

Big wicker basket *(above) is what every bunny needs. Gunther has renovated his, giving him a better view.* **Cardboard concrete form** *(above right) stimulates Jeffrey to run through it.* **Wicker tent** *(left) provides Ozzie with more action than just sitting inside.*

"Bunnies like the sound of paper ripping."

Phone directories for ripping (upper left)
Ball with tooth grippers for tossing (upper right)
Plastic rings to rattle and throw (lower left)
Stack of blocks to knock down and chin (lower right)

Newsprint paper is popular with rabbits. Though some of it may be chewed and swallowed, the main attraction is shredding. Bunnies like the sound of paper ripping.

Wooden chewables include well-dried tree branches or dried firewood with bark (check toxicity list on page 63). Also, non-toxic wooden blocks and other baby toys are safe for rabbits, as well as furring strips used for bunny-proofing baseboards.

Jingle-rattle toys are tossed, batted, and shaken. They include plastic balls with bells, car keys, and hard-plastic baby rattles. Rabbits are quite imaginative with noisy toys at 3:00 a.m. Jingly items remain popular with rabbits well into their senior

Photographs: upper left, Alison Geise; lower left, Judith Pierce

A basket of goodies (*left*) *provides Brit with plenty of choices to suit her fancy.*
Slinky management: Brit gives lessons on working a slinky (above). You pull it out of a basket and throw it over your shoulder.
Stretch it out: Butterscotch (below) shows how tall a slinky can stretch.

years. My old and severely disabled bunnies can still pick up their bells and balls and toss them from one place to another. Metal toys, after a few years of being urinated on or dunked in the water bowl, will eventually rust. Hard plastic toys can be washed repeatedly in hot soapy water and last for many generations.

Slinkies can come alive for rabbits as they do for game-playing humans. Rabbits like to pull them, shake them, and toss them. Put one in a box of assorted toys for your bunny to discover.

If you attach slinkies or other "loopy" toys to the side or top of the pen, make sure they detach easily, in case your bunny's foot becomes entangled.

Photographs: above and inset, Carolyn Long; lower right, Mary Cotter

Basket with handles:
Oliver (upper left) wears his creatively.
Cardboard house *not yet chewed: (upper right) gives Emy a place to hide.*
Cardboard box *already chewed: (lower left) Nim finishes trimming the last piece of a long project.*
Paper bag *(lower right) is good to check out before shredding.*

Some rabbit caregivers have discontinued all types of rigidly attached toys or hay hangers.

Cardboard as a box with cut-outs on the sides and top provides a hiding place, as well as a chewing project. It usually takes a few weeks for a rabbit to destroy a box, while having fun at the same time. Flat sheets of cardboard can serve as a floor covering that is scratchable and chewable.

Paper bags also have multiple uses. They can be hidden in or chewed and shredded. My rabbit Dickens was a notorious rug chewer until I started giving him brown grocery bags. He shreds them compulsively into tiny pieces. and we have no more holes in his rugs. ∎

Photographs: upper left, Jim Stoneburner; lower left, Amy Espie

Chapter Six

House Training

Bunnies of any age train themselves. Our job is to provide the tools and materials they need to accomplish this task.

WHEN OUR FIRST RABBIT began showing a preference for a corner of our kitchen for her toilet needs, I had no clue that rabbits would do such a thing. I had covered the entire kitchen floor with newspapers, but when I found I was only replacing one newspaper a day, it occurred to me to slide a tray under the newspaper.

That first rudimentary litter tray was replaced by real litterboxes for my succeeding bunnies. While training methods may vary for the individual, the universal considerations will be: location, number of litterboxes, and what to put in them.

Litterboxes: *How to promote their use*

*A **large box** in a corner of their space (above) invites Kirby and Rosey to share time chewing the hay. **Converted carrier** (right) is suitable for disabled bunnies Michelle and Allie, who need easy access. Some litterboxes also have a low entrance.*

WHILE YOUR BUNNY IS NEW in your house, you will probably confine him to one room or a pen until you have thoroughly bunny proofed other areas. This is a good time to start encouraging those good habits that you know he wants to form. You don't need to cover the entire floor with newspapers the way I did, but several litterboxes can have the same effect.

You and your bunny are usually in agreement as to location. Neither of you want the litterbox in the middle of a busy room or in the path of the front door. Off to the side, and preferably in a corner works best, but make sure it's convenient for a bunny to do the "right" thing.

You might consider having duplicate litterboxes and use a "redundant system." This means that you put down a fresh box at the same time that you pick up the soiled one. When you leave an empty space, where the litterbox should be, your bunny may decide to use the floor, because he knows that is the right location!

LITTERBOX STYLES

Litterboxes now come in many sizes, shapes, and in colors. You can find one that matches your decor. Bunnies don't seem particular about the color of box you choose.

The style of the litterbox is a matter of user preference and where it is needed—small enough to fit inside a cage or tall enough so that he is not urinating over the side of the box. Some are lower at the front, allowing disabled bunnies to enter.

MAKE THE LITTERBOX INVITING

The litterbox should be a happy place, never to be associated with punishment. Hay, straw, and other chewables entice bunnies into the box and

Photograph: upper, Carolyn Long

keep them there. Well-placed toys also encourage them to linger awhile in the box.

POSITIVE REINFORCEMENT

Reprimands have no place in bunny training and, in fact, greatly interfere by associating stress with the litterbox. Screaming and thrusting him into the litterbox will not improve his litterbox habits. Instead rely on enticements, and praise him in a mellow voice when he enters the box.

ADDITIONAL BOXES

Offer a sleeping box, if needed. Rabbits start using a litterbox because they like it. Some like it so much that they sleep in it. This is a harmless habit if you keep the litterbox clean. Otherwise you can offer an additional box with a pad for sleeping.

Add litterboxes when you expand bunny's starter space. It's better to start with too many rather than too few, until a preference emerges.

MARKING TERRITORY

Rabbits need to mark new territory with urine or feces in order to feel that they belong in that environment (more noticeable when there are multiple animals). To encourage training, give them plenty of litterboxes that they can dutifully "mark." The space on both sides of a see-through fence between competitive rabbits will always invite territorial marking. Put a litterbox on both sides of the fence.

Exuberant bunnies often like to mark new play areas immediately upon entrance. If you take them straight to a litterbox in the new area, they soon get the idea that the litterbox is the territory to mark, and they associate it with additional freedom. Within a few weeks, they'll make a beeline for the litterbox on their own.

A wide puppy pan with easy access (above) is used by Peaches in her Madison foster home. The litter used is a wood-fuel pellet for automated wood stoves. These pellets are safe, since they can't allow creosote build-up in a stove.
A small box is adequate for a small rabbit like Sinbad. His box contains only hay-covered newspaper.

Natural Routines

AS BUNNY MATURES AND CARVES out his own territory, his regular use of litterboxes should be a natural evolution of what he wants to do anyway. If your bunny is not becoming self-trained, you may be giving too much space too soon. Or you may not be making the litterbox(es) enticing enough. Good toilet habits may take several weeks or months to achieve, depending on maturity.

Don't expect a perfectly housetrained bunny at six weeks old. Even youngsters with well-established litterbox habits may lose them when they reach adolescence and become hormone-driven until after their spay/neuter surgery.

Post-adolescent spayed or neutered rabbits are generally easier to house train because they're more inclined to settle into a routine. Older rabbits have often disproved the notion that a rabbit must be young to be trainable.

A transitory loss of training may occur when introductions are taking place and courting rabbits are trying to impress each other. After they are well acquainted, they regain their former habits. Rabbit routines that do not include some degree of good toilet habits may indicate a health problem.

LITTERBOX MAINTENANCE

Your own routine will include litter cleanup. Safe litters for rabbits are made from relatively benign materials such as paper fiber, mountain grasses, wheat, and specially processed woods (with reduced phenols). You can find them listed on the HRS website.[1] Avoid highly aromatic softwood shavings (indicating high phenols), as well as clumping litters and dusty clays. Even litters that are known to be nontoxic can cause internal damage and should not be ingested.

Litters may vary, but there are basically three options for filling a litterbox:

1. ***Newspaper lining*** (about eight single sheets) is covered with a three-inch layer of hay or straw.
2. ***Litter lining*** (one–two inches of litter) is covered by two–three inches of hay.
3. ***Litter or shredded paper*** is used alone, but an enticing treat or toy is added in one corner.

The third option is the most desirable during times of hay shortages, such as droughts or floods.

Paper-lined boxes that do not contain absorbent litter will need to be changed daily; the litter-lined boxes can go two days or more. For boxes shared with cats, keep any hay in a hanger or basket instead of on the floor of the litterbox. The way you manage litterboxes in your house will depend on the users. ∎

Pans within the habitats: (above) Honey's litterbox at the Rabbit Center is filled with pelleted grass litter topped with a layer of hay. Boxes are changed every other day using the "redundant" system.
Pan within starter space: (right) Jewel's litterbox is filled with pelleted grass litter only. This makes it possible to scoop out a small soiled area at a time between regular cleanings.

1. HRS Educators, "What Types of Litter Should I Use?" HRS website, http://rabbit.org/faq-litter-training-2/

Behavior: An all-too-brief introduction

By Mary Cotter, Ed.D, LVT

ONE OF THE GREATEST JOYS of living with companion rabbits is getting to watch the incredibly rich variety of behaviors they exhibit when housed in a familiar and comfortable indoor environment, where they feel safe enough to let their guard down. They explore, they climb, they leap, they chew, they dig, they build, they destroy, they dance, they roll, they flop—and then they start all over again.

Rabbit behavior is endlessly fascinating, but can also be frustrating when some behaviors become "problems."

Three topics account for the vast majority of behavior questions addressed to HRS and probably also for the vast majority of shelter relinquishments: "inappropriate" urination, "destructiveness," and "aggression."

"What can I do about behavior problems?"

First, be aware that "problem" behaviors (except those caused by medical conditions) may be natural, "hard-wired" behaviors. Understanding a rabbit's basic needs, and adjusting the environment to meet them, can usually significantly reduce the problem behavior or completely resolve it.

House training is a case in point. When you make it easy for the rabbit to do the right thing by providing him with strategically placed litterboxes, filled with appropriate litter material (such as grass hay), you protect your own property while simultaneously offering the rabbit the opportunity to eliminate in a manner that feels "right" to him.

"My rabbit was litter-trained but is suddenly peeing outside his box!"

Any sudden behavior change, particularly when it is related to physiological functions such as eating and eliminating, warrants a vet visit to rule out underlying medical problems. Sudden litterbox changes, for example, may indicate a urinary tract infection, spinal arthritis, or even generalized pain.

If no medical causes are found, your rabbit may have "marked" areas outside his litterbox, and is returning to those spots. Enzymatic cleaners can help, but removing his access to those spots is probably the most effective thing you can do. If the rabbit is urinating just outside the litterbox, try placing the litterbox inside an even larger box, or on a piece of washable, rubber backed carpet.

"My bunny is destroying everything in my house!"

Rabbits are chewers by nature, and need a carefully rabbit-proofed environment with objects to chew that are safe and entertaining. Wooden or cardboard chew toys or boxes, small unpainted furniture—all can be bought or made, and greatly help to enrich your rabbit's environment. Many rabbits love to chew against resistance (such as woodwork, wallpaper, table legs). For these rabbits, tacking a furring strip over your woodwork protects the woodwork and provides the rabbit something safe to gnaw on. Restrict your rabbit's access to anything you do not want "sampled:" confining him in a spacious puppy exercise pen when you are not there to supervise is a great way to do this. In summary, it is much easier to find ways to accommodate your rabbit's natural tendencies than to eliminate them.

"My rabbit used to be friendly but now she is aggressive!"

Most humans try to avoid judging other people, yet we judge our companion animals all the time. We label their behavior with words that are simply mental

A spunky attitude qualifies Goober as "endlessly fascinating," but if his behavior becomes a problem, he asks not to be pre-judged.

"An effective way to change this behavior is to change the associations your rabbit has with your hands."

Personality disorder?
Lewis will be the first to inform you that labels don't tell you anything about what is going on in the rabbit's mind.

constructs—conclusions we have drawn about presumed "underlying causes." Compare, for example, these two descriptions: "My rabbit is mean and aggressive" *vs:* "When I reach my hand into my rabbit's cage, she moves quickly to the back corner and then lunges and boxes at my hand; and if I keep moving my hand toward her, she bites me."

The first description involves labels and judgments about the underlying "personality disorder" of the rabbit, and gives us no information about what the rabbit is actually doing or under what conditions she is doing it. The second description tells us exactly what can be observed, and under what conditions it is happening. This allows us to focus on those conditions and change them, in order to change the behavior.

If your rabbit has recently reached sexual maturity, spaying her will remove the hormones that may be influencing her behavior.

But it's important to look beyond hormones in this situation, and to ask: under what conditions am I seeing this "hormonal" behavior? The behavior occurs when you reach your hands into her cage to take her out. Many rabbits associate hands with being lifted, which most do not like. As you move your hand toward your rabbit, she does her best to warn you (by boxing, lunging, grunting) that she wants you to back off. If you continue to advance, you make clear to her that her "early warning signals" will be disregarded, and you leave her no alternative but to bite.

An effective way to change this behavior is to change the associations your rabbit has with your hands, so that your hands come to predict pleasant events, rather than unpleasant ones. When you open her cage door, instead of reaching in to grab her, place a yummy treat on the cage floor just inside the door, and then back off, so that she feels safe to come to the front. Do this each day until she comes forward readily when you enter her area. With patience on your part, eventually, she will be willing to take the treat directly from your hand, and you will not need to back off.

At the same time, offer her a way to exit her cage that does not require being grasped by you. If her cage is elevated, consider putting it on the floor, so she can exit it herself. Alternatively, put a treat in her carrier, to entice her into that. Or hold a hay-filled litterbox just outside the cage door until she steps into it. Above all, be patient; fear and discomfort do not dissolve overnight.

"Where can I learn more about behavior?"

In the past quarter century, behavioral science has produced an enormous body of research on the technology of behavior change, called "Applied Behavior Analysis." ABA is now being used more and more widely by animal caretakers, thanks largely to the vision of Susan Friedman, Ph.D., a psychologist who has pioneered the application of ABA to captive and companion animals. Her articles (www.behaviorworks.org) focus on parrots, but the principles she discusses are general ones that can be used with any species and are particularly helpful for working with prey species, such as rabbits. For rabbit-specific behavior, Ann McBride's book, *Why Does My Rabbit?,* is excellent. ∎

Mary Cotter, Ed.D, LVT, *is founder of Rabbit Rescue and Rehab of NYC and producer of the video* Rabbit Handling and Nail-cutting.

Photograph: Mary Cotter

Chapter Seven

7

Bonding
Rabbits have intense social needs that make living in isolation notably unnatural.

WHEN RABBITS LIVE NATURALLY in groups, they often have a favorite friend or two. Therefore living in pairs in your home is also a happy arrangement. Before they are introduced, all parties must be spayed or neutered at least one month prior to the introduction.

Though intrinsically sociable, many rabbits have not yet discovered this fact and can be difficult to bond. Caregivers have varying experiences as to what makes the best match. My own introductions are based on individual personalities, without much attention to gender, breed, or size. I do, however, consider their state of health and physical needs.

Photograph: Jim Stoneburner

Introductions: *Long and short*

Sources of contention *might be some desirable territory (above). Peggy Sue and Jasmine vie over the occupation of a prized cardboard house.*
Compromised? *(lower right) Best buddies, Chester and Max, are so comfortable with each other that they don't notice disabilities.*

WHETHER YOUR INTENDED PARTNERS are housed in separate pens within the same room or in separate rooms, the important thing is that when they do come together it is in territory that neither has claimed before.

GET-ACQUAINTED SESSIONS

Set up a pen with a litterbox and maybe a few toys. Keep your own supplies nearby: a dustpan and a squirt bottle filled with plain water. Put the bunnies and yourself into the pen. Make the first few sessions short—about ten minutes once or twice a day for healthy rabbits. For compromised rabbits make the sessions about five minutes.

Sit with the bunnies for the entire session for the first few days, giving them your undivided attention. Don't allow a pattern of fighting. If they're not ready to play nice on any given day, then separate them until the next day or later the same day.

Hold a squirt bottle, set to "stream" and be ready to use it. Keep in spraying distance at all times, and if one rabbit starts to growl and attack the other, give him a squirt right in the face. He/she will take time out to face wash. This triggers some very interesting behavior. When you see newly introduced rabbits simply occupying the same territory, ignoring each other but nervously grooming themselves, you can bet that within a day or two, they will be grooming each other.

You can also induce extra licking/grooming behavior by scratching the "tickle" spots on the lower spine that cause them to lick. You can pet both bunnies vigorously from head to tail. This gives them something to think about other than an adversary and keeps them used to being handled.

After observing who likes to groom and who likes to be groomed, you can smear a sticky treat of applesauce or mashed banana on the head of the bunny who enjoys being groomed.

MOUNTING BEHAVIOR

Rabbits will circle and mount each other regardless of neutering. This is not an attack but part of the normal introductory process. Mounting is preferable to fighting.

If the mounting behavior becomes too rough, put the dustpan between them (do NOT separate with your hands). Sometimes a rabbit mounts another backwards. This may be seductive foreplay, but it can turn risky if the rabbit underneath decides to start biting the genitals of the rabbit on top. Any time you see backwards mounting, you must intervene to protect the top bunny from severe injury.

INCREASE SESSION TIME

As soon as the bunnies are able to tolerate each other for a full twenty minutes with you inside the pen, you can begin to stay outside the pen but nearby with the water bottle. In the next few days, you can begin "multi-tasking"—go about your business within hearing distance.

Photograph: lower, Margo DeMello

Increase the pen time until the bunnies can be together most of the day. They may sit on opposite sides of the pen at first, and then gradually sit close and snuggle during the day. After showing this cordial behavior for a few days, they are ready to remain together at night. The whole process takes about five weeks, unless your bunnies have had a head start with an introduction at the shelter.

LAP SESSIONS

For bunnies who are people friendly, try spreading your own good rapport among the bunnies. This works well for disabled rabbits and is also a good supplement to other techniques. You can do the sessions alone or with help.

Two people: Sit side-by-side on a sofa with a bunny on each lap with bunnies' faces about three inches apart. Each person strokes the bunny and talks soothingly.

One person: Sit on a sofa with a bunny on each side of you. Have both sets of forepaws on your lap. Stroke each bunny simultaneously. You might try this while watching TV or listening to music—anything that doesn't engage your hands.

INTRODUCING COMPROMISED RABBITS

While many animals carry subclinical diseases that never cause them or their partners a problem, we don't want to load too much stress all at once on an immune system that may be fighting such a disease. Even though friendship, once achieved, supports longevity, the process of becoming friends can be stressful. Therefore we use caution with older, chronically ill, or in any way compromised animals. Disabled bunnies are perfect candidates for "lap sessions," since they are already accustomed to human handling. Most show no stress whatsoever. And surprisingly, many rabbits in advancing years may accept partners who would have been intolerable at an earlier time.

BELONGING TO A GROUP

Living in trios or small groups (four–six) is ideal for most rabbits in private homes. Sanctuaries, on the other hand, usually house twenty or more in a large group that structures itself into a hierarchy, with chiefs and queens and adoring subjects. Large groups may form smaller sub-groups with mini-hierarchies. Even so, a few individuals are ill-suited to the social pressure of large communal living but are quite happy with one or two low-key friends. Groups are formed and expanded several ways:

All at once: A large number of individual rabbits are introduced in a large space with human monitors nearby to prevent fighting.

Three newcomers at a time are introduced under supervision to a large group. We don't try to introduce a single rabbit at a time, because of the stress of being the sole object of nudging, prodding, mounting, and being picked on by the others.[1]

A single rabbit is introduced to a bonded pair, a trio, or small group. This is time consuming! The newcomer is bonded individually to each member of the group, before they can all be put together. I've made two exceptions to this rule, by placing a fourth rabbit with certain non-aggressive trios. ∎

A happy trio (above): Usani, Eva, and Annabelle live at Harvest Home Animal Sanctuary in Stockton, CA, where the occupants are able to choose their own friends.

---

1. Karen Courtemanche, "Keeping the Peace." Master Seminar 2 (2010). DVD: see page 94

Another Bonding Perspective

BY BETH WOOLBRIGHT

Beginning period of an introduction requires close supervision. The bunnies' body language indicates the degree of tension.

AT THE RABBIT CENTER, in Richmond, California, a fair number of our placements are to single rabbits previously adopted from the Center who come back with their guardians looking to add another (spayed/neutered) rabbit to the mix. In general, humans make lousy rabbit matchmakers; so when possible, let your bunny do the choosing. (Frankly, I think the reason rabbits copulate so quickly is because otherwise, chances are, they'll fight.)

At this shelter, we use speed dating, where the bunny looking for a companion is introduced, one at a time, to three or four possible matches, with bunnies usually of the opposite sex. While boy-boy combinations can work, girls who were not raised together don't usually get along.

The two rabbits, with a human chaperone, are put in an X-pen or other small space that's neutral territory with a clean litterbox that has both litter and hay. (Bunnies seem to find munching hay comforting.)

Have some device to aid in separating them if there's serious fighting. We use a dustpan to put between them, if necessary. I keep the litterbox in the space for the first 10 or 20 minutes so the bunny pairing has a home base where they can retreat and regroup. After that it's removed to reduce territorial behavior.

To some degree bondings rely on the skill of the person overseeing the introduction—and knowing when to intervene. Some mounting, chasing, or boxing is a normal part of the process. If things start to escalate, my method is to put the two side-by-side and stroke both bunnies firmly from head to tail. This helps them know they can calmly occupy the same space. The primary rule is keep things positive and pleasant.

Know this: love at first sight is rare. If you think about it, most rabbits haven't seen another bunny since being removed from their brothers and sisters, so their social skills may need coaxing. Rabbits also don't give their friendship away freely; thus, once a likely match is found, we require three dates to see how it goes. The first one can be about 20 minutes. On successive dates, offer vegetables to the two, again for that positive experience. While grooming is the hoped-for goal, some sparring or even simple peaceful co-existence may result in (good) sparks later.

When we decide we have a match, the pair go home together in the same carrier. There's something about car rides that seems to break down the animosity between rabbits and enhances the process. Even then, it may take weeks of supervised dating before the bunnies make their love connection and can be left alone together. ∎

Beth Woolbright *is a founding and current board member of the National House Rabbit Society, a supervisor at the Rabbit Center, and a staff editor for the* House Rabbit Journal.

Photograph: Tania Harriman

Feline Friends

Many people who adopt rabbits already have cats. If your new bunny comes into a house with several cats, you may find that entirely different relationships build between individuals. No special step-by-step introductory process is required other than to intervene if one or the other becomes aggressive.

Household cats don't normally view adult rabbits as prey, but don't allow your cat access to a very young bunny (rat size). And lively, playful kittens, with their needle-sharp claws and teeth, can be dangerous to rabbits of any age. So monitoring is necessary for all kittens. Post-adolescent cats require less supervision around rabbits, but cats of all ages should have their nails trimmed very short.

Sometimes a bold rabbit may try to bully a cat, but more often it's a matter of sniffing and nudging, and trying to get the cat's attention. None of the rabbits in my house have ever been afraid of our cats, and they all seem to decide for themselves what kind of interaction they will have.

CO-EXISTING RELATIONSHIP

The least interactive relationship between a cat and a rabbit is simply a co-existence, which is nevertheless a positive experience. They are entertained by watching the other's activities, and they may even doze off in a nearby location or sit in close proximity.

PLAYFUL RELATIONSHIP

While providing delightful experiences for both the cat and the bunny, especially in their youth, a playful relationship requires the most monitoring and regular inspections by the caregiver. Although cats quite often swat at their friends with their claws retracted, sometimes they do not. Keeping the nails short prevents deep penetration, but you also need to check for bite wounds. Cats sometimes bite their friends in play.

Be ready to treat any surface scratches and wounds. Often it means immediately disinfecting a small area and applying antibiotic ointment. Watch closely for infection (swelling and heat), which may require a visit to your vet and treatment with systemic antibiotics.

INTIMATE RELATIONSHIP

Individual cats and rabbits can develop extraordinary rapport and spend a lot of time in close physical contact. This most often happens in multi-animal households, where individuals have a greater selection of potential friends and can choose their own companions.

Our cat Octavia became a "nurse" when her friend Phoebe was sick. Octavia's around-the-clock comfort and moral support contributed as much to Phoebe's recovery as the medicine I gave her. ∎

Whispering sweet nothings in Octavia's ear (above), Phoebe professes her everlasting devotion.
Simultaneous caresses: Rob rests his chin on Daphne's head (below), while Daphne snuggles her head under Rob's chin.

Photograph: lower, Amy Espie

Dogs and Bunnies

MORE IMPORTANT THAN DOG or bunny behavior in establishing a compatible relationship is human behavior. Our job is to show our dogs how we want them to behave around our rabbits. Dog training is the best guarantee of safety for your rabbit. While you may plan to keep the animals separated by a gate or door, training your dog is insurance against disaster if that door is accidentally left open.

LEARNING COMMANDS

Your dog must first be responsive to the basic human commands: "down-stay," "good dog," "gentle," and "off." Since it's absolutely crucial that the dog not chase if the rabbit runs, you must start with the following preventive setup.

1. Dog is in a puppy pen when bunnies have free run. Curious rabbits can observe an unthreatening dog, who is contained in a pen. Free-running rabbits can be observed by the dog in a non-chase setting.

2. Bunnies are in pen/cage when the dog has free run. The rabbits gradually become accustomed to the noises, smells, and strange movements of the dog. They can sniff noses and get acquainted through the safety of the wire fencing.

3. Dog is on leash when all are out of pens. Gradually have short sessions with a short leash and lots of praise when the dog behaves well among the rabbits.

5. Daily dog-style play to expend energy away from

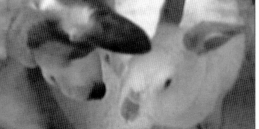

Nose-to-nose nuzzles: Xena dog and Jefty rabbit find pleasure in each other's company.

bunnies: running, jumping, and fetching a ball.

When we brought home our eight-month-old Australian shepherd, Xena, we started with the previously described steps, and then added:

6. Participation in duties off leash. Xena began to make the rounds with us as we gave nightly feedings to the bunnies. As we talked gently, filled dishes, and stroked the bunnies, Xena mimicked our manner with gentle grooming.

7. Build on praise more than reprimand. Xena's experience with rabbits was kept positive. Dog trainer Amy Espie had advised us to avoid situations that were known to cause frustration and introduced us in 1992 to a fundamental called "setting up for success."[2]

8. Co-mingling in our presence. We took down the puppy pen and allowed Xena freedom of the house. Not wanting to risk a sudden overwhelming impulse of a young playful pup, we never left her alone with the rabbits during the first year.

As she spent more and more time freely commingling with rabbits in our presence, we began to leave them together for short periods during their quiet times of day.

PATIENCE PAYS OFF

After another six unhurried months, we were rewarded with free running rabbits living comfortably with a young dog, who no longer required supervision and could be left alone with the rabbits for an indeterminate period of time. Read Amy's online article[3] for additional consideration. ■

2. Amy (Shapiro) Espie, "Rebel with Paws," *House Rabbit Journal* II, no. 9 (1992), http://rabbit.org/rebel-with-paws/

3. ———. "When Fido Met Thumper," *House Rabbit Journal* I, no. 4 (1989) http://rabbit.org/when-fido-met-thumper-dogs-and-rabbits-2/

Training Aggressive Dogs to be Rabbit Friendly

YES, IT CAN BE DONE. Through careful dog training and monitoring, an aggressive dog can live among rabbits. It does require extra commitment, more patience, additional time, and cooperation of all family members.

In 2011, Bill and Amy Harriman and their three sons, Aladdin, Nico, and Rian, scattered the ashes of their beloved dog Baran in a mountain meadow where the family camps. Baran, a lab-pit mix, was an extraordinary example of a vicious dog who had learned to modify his behavior around the three family rabbits, Tails, Sonic, and Knuckles. With a history of attacking everyone except immediate family members, Baran had been quarantined twice by Animal Control and was not considered a safe prospect to hang out with rabbits.

COMPLICATED GOALS

Adding to the difficulty, the family wanted Baran and the rabbits to play outside at the same time. Away from the easier setting of the quiet indoors, they were trying to instill gentleness with rabbits in a rambunctious dog in the wide-open space of their large backyard. Also in the mix was their old, mellow dog, Peppy. But their focus was on training Baran, since Peppy always followed Baran's lead.

The family devised this plan and stuck to it:

1. *A large wire-mesh bunny enclosure* allows the dogs to see and sniff and provides enough room for rabbits to move away when they tire of the sniffing.

2. *Vocal communication* is essential. Reprimand excitability, but more often praise calm behavior.

3. *Repeat exposure daily* until the dog can walk calmly over to the bunny pen.

4. *When a daily pattern of calmness* is established, try the dog in a stationary location on a short leash and muzzle while bunnies run loose.

5. *One person holds dog* while one places bunny in the yard. This "authorizes" the rabbit to be there.

6. *If dog whines* or tries to lunge when bunnies pass by, hold back sternly. When calm praise lavishly.

7. *Repeat sessions* in one location until dog shows calm behavior pattern with free-running rabbits.

8. *Start daily walks with dog on leash* and muzzle into bunny play area, repeating reprimands for lunging and praise for not lunging.

9. *When calm behavior is established,* allow still-muzzled dog off leash in bunny area for several days.

10. *When a pattern of calmness is set,* have two or more people monitor first few un-muzzled off-leash meetings of dog and bunnies.

After all the weeks of training and preparation, the off-leash meeting was a non-event. The behavior of the dog and rabbits was already in place.

GOALS ACHIEVED

The desire to have both species run freely in the backyard had finally been fulfilled, and in fact, the bunnies' playtime was made safer with Baran's protection. Local wildlife kept their distance.

When I visited the backyard playground several months later, I saw for myself how far Baran had come. When Tails and Sonic get into a scuffle, Baran ran over to them and put one paw on Sonic's shoulder, stopping the fight. I was stunned. Baran was not only a protector but also a peacekeeper! ■

Patio activities: Sonic finds a carrot to munch, while smiling Baran peruses the outer yard.

Guinea Pig Pals

BECAUSE GUINEA PIGS have a delicate respiratory system that can be infected by bacteria carried by other animals, many veterinarians advise against housing them with rabbits. On the other hand, a large number of guinea pigs are living healthy and happy lives with rabbits, and the veterinarians who treat them never encounter problems from cohabitation.

Guinea pigs in the community, as well as the rabbits, should be spayed or neutered. An guinea pig, when un-altered, might be so driven to mount and chase that he/she might cause a rabbit to become aggressive. Hormones and overcrowding are two major causes of aggression. Forcing a rabbit and guinea pig together in a small cage, understandably, is inviting trouble. Both species need plenty of room for free roaming so they can go about their activities and not feel overwhelmed by the other.

If you can't let them run freely in a large space all the time, an alternative is to provide them with separate sleeping quarters for night time and a large play area for daytime use. When my daughter, Tania, let Hank and Gordon out to run freely in the

Cordial encounters between piggy Hank and bunny Nibble highlight their friendly relationship.

morning, they would head straight to Phoebe's hangout (page 11). She loved their company.

If you let your guinea pigs have run of the house, even part time, you need to put a lot of little flat trays along the edges of the rooms they use. Another place they may designate as a "bathroom" is under the bed. We discovered this one time as we pulled out a flat storage box and found it had been converted to a guinea pig litterbox.

THINGS THEY CAN SHARE

When rabbits and guinea pigs share a playground, you can give them the same kind of toys, such as dried wood, but give them species-specific lounging areas, such as small tents, tepees, and hiding boxes for guinea pig respite. A platform/mezzanine or an elevated cot allows a quiet place for when a bunny tires of noisy guinea pig chatter.

Although rabbits and guinea pigs can share chew toys and have similar tastes, their dietary needs are quite different. Guinea pigs require a daily intake of vitamin C, whereas rabbits do not. They need to be singled out and fed separately a large quantity of leafy veggies, bell peppers, oranges, tomatoes, and other foods rich in vitamin C.

Diet information, based largely on hay, will soon be published for guinea pigs and other small animals.[4] Guinea pigs are similar to rabbits in their sensitivity to certain antibiotics. Your rabbit-savvy veterinarian will be familiar with both species.

Rabbits can also interact with another improbable species, as described by Julie Smith.[5] ∎

---

4. Judy Hardin, *Dining at the Leaf and Twig Cafe: The Hay-Intensive Diet for Pet Rabbits, Guinea Pigs and Chinchillas.* (2013) Check website for availability, http://www.rabbitears.org
5. Julie Smith, "When Worlds Collide," *House Rabbit Journal* IV, no. 8 (2003), http://rabbit.org/worlds.

Chapter Eight

Rabbit Nutrition

What to feed your rabbit is based on both nutritional and functional needs.

8

ABBITS ARE VORACIOUS EATERS and, like their wild cousins, can consume large quantities of organic material. Wild rabbits eat succulent grass in the spring, dried grass or straw later in the year. They eat cultivated crops grown for feedstuffs and garden vegetables grown for humans. They eat the fruit that falls from trees, as well as bark from the trees themselves.

All rabbits love to forage. This is built into their survival instinct. Feeding your house rabbit is more than meeting nutritional requirements. You are feeding a little psyche—not only in a bowl but also by stashing those high-bulk, low-calorie chewables around the house for bunny to find. That's part of the program.

Photograph: Bob Harriman

Food Sources: *Select from a variety*

Long stem parsley (above) is destined to disappear in Oliver's presence.
***Hay, straw**, and large leafy greens are served up on a sea grass rug (lower left).*
***Dandelion greens** (lower right) are ready for harvest at the Rabbit Center, where organic veggies are grown in surrounding planters for the shelter bunnies.*

NUTRITION IS PROVIDED through varieties of foods that deliver bunnies' minimum requirements of protein, carbohydrate, fat, fiber, vitamins, and minerals, along with necessary calories in the following percentages:[1]

Protein 12%   Carbohydrate 50%

Fat 3%   Digested fiber 35%

As hindgut fermenters, rabbits get their digested-fiber calories through the fermentation process (detailed in the next chapter).

FIBER: DIGESTIBLE AND INDIGESTIBLE

In addition to digestible organic material, your bunny needs a large quantity of indigestible fiber to stimulate gut motility. Hay provides both kinds of fiber. Grass hays, such as timothy, bluegrass, orchard hay, and ryegrass, are usually best for mature rabbits. Alfalfa and clover hays, which are higher in calcium and protein, are better for growing rabbits.

However, hay is so critical to good health that it's better to feed even mature rabbits alfalfa and clover-based hays, rather than no hay at all.

Choose long-strand hays to obtain the maximum fiber benefit. Nutritional values in dried hays vary greatly with the soil conditions and the season and the cut—making it difficult to meet all nutrient requirements consistently with hay alone.

Hay quality and edibility also depend on good storage. Keep all hay stored in a cool dry place. Dampness can allow mold growth, which can be lethal to a rabbit by altering gut flora.

FRESH PRODUCE

Veggies: Most of what you find in the produce section of the supermarket is OK for your rabbit, with a few exceptions. Avoid starchy vegetables

1. Susan Smith, "Rabbit Nutrition in Health and Disease." Master Seminar 3 (2010). DVD: See page 94.

Photograph: upper left, Jim Stoneburner; others, by author

(raw or cooked), such as beans, corn, peas, potatoes, as these can cause digestive upset. Do offer a variety of vegetables and include a range of lettuces, fresh herbs, brassicas (broccoli family), and other greens. Some rabbits have sensitivities to certain vegetables, so test them one at a time when introducing them into your rabbit's diet.

Never offer a rabbit raw beans, potato peels, rhubarb, or any scraps that are too old to eat yourself. Spoiled food might make you sick, but it could also kill your rabbit.

Fruit: Fresh apples, bananas, berries, grapes, melons, pears, peaches, plums, pineapples, and papayas are favorites with rabbits. Avoid citrus.

While some veterinarians discourage the use of any fruit whatsoever, others may allow it if fed sparingly (a small slice daily) and if the bunny's digestive tract tolerates fruit. It's better to keep it

limited, even when well tolerated, since the extra sugar can result in an overweight rabbit. I find a banana slice useful for camouflaging oral medications. Dried fruit is even more concentrated than fresh fruit, so the quantity should be more limited (e.g. one dried sweetened cranberry).

PELLETED FEED

Pellets were developed for livestock, with an emphasis on rapid weight gain, but some manufacturers today produce "maintenance" varieties for our non-breeding house rabbits. Pellet ingredients are listed on the bag as percentages of protein, fiber, and additional vitamins and minerals—in order of abundance. Calories, or digestible energy (DE), are not always listed. For a healthy, mature rabbit, look for a pellet that is higher in fiber (20% or more), lower in protein (12–14%), and lower in calcium (0.8–1.2%).

A juicy strawberry (above) is thoroughly enjoyed by shelter bunny Herbie.
Hay and succulent greens *(lower left) are daily offerings for Jasimine, a disabled bunny who also eats wet pellets (page 60).*
Pellet bowls *are for resting a chin (lower right) when one tires of munching.*

Foraging fun (upper): *Cumin and Buster find their favorite snacks in a pile of hay and greens.* **Bedtime treat** (right): *Nolan eagerly stands up for his apple slice.*

Most high-fiber pellets are made with grass hay instead of alfalfa. But a few alfalfa-based pellets have been developed also that are lower in protein and higher in fiber.

Avoid pellets that contain whole seeds, grains and dried vegetables, because these are calorie-rich, and many rabbits learn to prefer them at the expense of other foods.

When given in excess, all pellets can cause obesity, but in small amounts, they provide important vitamins, minerals, and essential fatty acids. Different pellets are appropriate for different needs.

CONCENTRATED TREATS

Most bunnies can tolerate a pinch or two of oats or barley or a single dried berry. Avoid crackers, seeds, nuts, and fried banana, which are high in starch, sugars, or fats. As you will see in the next chapter, excesses starch and sugar can cause very serious illness. ■

Table 1. *Energy, protein, fiber, and calcium in several feedstuffs per one-ounce servings*

FRESH PRODUCE	DRY MAT. (%)	ENERGY (calories)	PROTEIN (%)	PROTEIN (g)	FIBER (%)	FIBER (g)	CALCIUM (%)	CALCIUM (mg)
Apple	21	20	0.5	.1	1.2	.3	.01	3
Banana	24	24	1.1	.3	.5	.1	.01	3
Broccoli	9.3	8.0	3.0	0.8	1.1	0.3	.05	13
Cabbage	12	8	2.2	.6	2.0	0.6	.08	23
Carrot tops	17	—	2.7	.8	1.9	0.5	.32	91
Carrots	12	14	1.2	.3	1.1	0.3	.04	11
Celery	6	4	0.9	.3	.6	0.2	.04	11
Chard, swiss	7.3	5.6	1.8	0.5	0.8	0.24	0.05	15
Cilantro	7.2	7.0	2.4	0.7	0.8	0.21	0.1	28
Collards	9.4	5.3	1.6	0.44	0.6	0.16	9.12	33
Dandelion greens	15	8	2.8	.8	1.7	0.5	.20	57
Endive	6.2	4.0	1.25	0.3	0.9	0.35	0.05	13
Kale	15	9	3.1	.9	2.0	0.6	.24	68
Lettuce, green	5	3	1.2	.3	.6	0.2	.05	14
Parsley	11.6	11.0	3.0	0.9	1.2	0.36	.09	41
Spinach	8.4	6.0	2.7	0.8	2.5	0.7	0.1	28
HAYS & GRAINS								
Alfalfa hay	90	51	15.3	4.3	27.0	7.7	1.35	383
Bermuda grass hay	92	47	11.0	3.1	27.6	7.8	.38	108
Clover hay red	88	50	17.3	4.9	21.8	6.2	1.28	364
Clover hay white	92	58	21.4	6.1	20.9	5.9	1.75	497
Lespedeza hay	92	37	12.7	3.6	28.1	8.0	.92	261
Oats grain	90	77	11.1	3.2	11.3	3.2	.03	9
Oat hay	88	57	7.3	2.1	29.5	8.4	.25	71
Orchard grass fresh	27	15	3.8	1.1	6.9	2.0	.07	20
Prairie hay	92	47	5.3	1.5	31.0	8.8	.0	0
Ryegrass hay	89	59	3.8	1.1	33.0	9.4	.45	128
Sunflower seeds	92	94	17.1	4.9	22.3	6.3	.20	57
Timothy hay	80	57	6.3	1.8	30.2	8.6	.20	57
Wheat straw	89	38	3.2	.9	37.0	10.5	.15	43

Sources

Table 1 *is adapted from* Rabbit Feeding and Nutrition *(Cheeke 1987) with specifically rabbit values and* United States-Canadian Tables of Feed Composition *(not necessarily for rabbits)*

Diet Plans for Healthy Rabbits

D IETARY NEEDS for most species change during a lifetime. Any diet plan should be appropriate to age, health conditions, metabolism and tolerances of the individual. The plan should combine the food selection with suggested amounts to meet adequate nutrition requirements. Since rabbits can extract 35% of their daily calorie requirement from hay, the rest of the energy and nutrients must come from other foods.

Table 2. *Minimal Metabolic Requirements for Rabbits to Maintain Optimum Body Weight* [2]

Body wt lbs	2	3	4	5	6	7	8	9	10
Calories	89	120	149	170	202	227	251	274	296

THE YOUNG DIET

Take extra care with weanlings, under seven weeks old, to keep their food clean. (For hand feeding orphan babies see chapter 10.) This is a transition period, in which the sterile intestines are being introduced to bacteria. All rabbits must establish healthy intestinal flora during this time in order to survive. But they can't do it all at once. Watch for sensitivity to a particular food by adding only one new food at time.

Table 3. *Beginner Diets: Babies and "Teenagers"*

Birth to 2 weeks: Mother's milk
2–4 weeks: Mother's milk, nibbles of alfalfa hay, pellets, well washed greens—introduced one at a time (Orphans: baby food starter, see page 85)
4–7 weeks: Mother's milk, unlimited alfalfa hay and pellets (for kids and mom), clean veggies/fruit—add one at a time
7 weeks–7 months: Unlimited alfalfa hay and pellets, additional veggies/fruit—one at a time
7 months–1 year: Introduce grass and oat hays, gradually eliminate alfalfa, gradually limit pellets, expand variety of fresh produce

THE ADULT DIET

Once your rabbit is fully grown, you need to figure out how much to feed of what. Most veterinarians and rabbit-nutrition experts agree that hay should be the largest part of the adult-rabbit diet.

If your rabbit is reluctant to eat the hay that's available to her at all times, try having two different kinds available alternately. This way you can give fresh offerings of one kind then the other, or even fresh offerings of the same hay. When I come around in the afternoon, and offer my rabbits the same kind of hay that they're sitting on, they grab it from my hand like it's a big deal.

Table 4. *Daily Diet for Mature Rabbits*

Grass hay: Unlimited. Encourage at least 2 large handfuls.
Vegetables: A heaping cup chopped or 2 large handfuls.
Fresh fruit: 1–2 tbsp (e.g. ⅛ of a small apple or a thin slice of banana) daily or occasionally, if bunny is not overweight and tolerates it well
Pellets: ¼ cup daily depending on pellet density and bunny's weight. This ensures trace amounts of vital nutrients.

Because pellets range widely in their caloric content, the serving size may need to adjusted to arrive at your rabbit's optimum weight. Generally, smaller rabbits need more food per pound than do larger rabbits. A good way to track your bunny's weight gain is shown on page 62.

According to nutritionist Susan Smith (who has provided a substantial amount of the information in this chapter), adequate nutrition is hard to achieve with no pellets at all. You must give five–seven different veggies daily and a variety of hays.[3]

Parsley sprigs *are the greens of preference for Cupcake O'Neill.*

2. P. R. Cheeke, "Maintenance Requirements of New Zealand Whites," *Rabbit Feeding and Nutrition*: 70-71 (1987)
3. Susan Smith, "Rabbit Nutrition." Master Seminar 3 (2010)

Special Diet Planning

A leafy endeavor (above): Theodore engages himself in a large chewing project. **Fortified pellet mush** *is served to disabled Nika (lower right) in a small accessible dish.*

STAGE OF LIFE and physical conditions affect what your bunny eats and how he is fed. Sometimes it's a matter of making the meals accessible for immobile rabbits, or softer for rabbits with dental problems, or higher in protein for long-haired rabbits. It may be specifically designed by your vet as part of a treatment plan.

HYDRATION AS WELL AS NUTRITION

We can usually count on healthy rabbits to consume enough fluid for their needs. However, their needs can be become elevated due to urinary disease. Dr. Carolynn Harvey devised the following high-fluid diet for our bunnies who had undergone bladder-stone surgery and needed to keep their urine diluted (USG under 1.010).

Table 5. *Daily Diet for Diluting Urine*

Leafy greens: 4 large handfuls	
Root/stalk (carrot, celery, broccoli): 4 oz	
Fresh fruit (e.g. apple slice): ½ oz	
Grass hay: Unlimited	
Wet pellets: 1 tbsp	

I use the above diet for many of my aging rabbits, who can't always access their water source and could become dehydrated. For this reason, I want all their food, other than hay, to be wet. Various health conditions may require food to be pulverized in addition to being wet. This can be done easily with Oxbow Critical Care, or you can mix your own pellet mush.

Recipe for Pellet Mush

> *Finely grind ¼ cup pellets in a coffee grinder*
> *Add 2 tbsp canned pumpkin or baby food puree*
> *Add enough water for mushy consistency*

The mush mixture is fine enough to spoon into a 35cc feeding syringe from your vet. Use several syringes, partially filled, for easy plunging. A single feeding for a six-pound rabbit is about 50cc.

While some convalescing or disabled bunnies may continue to require syringe feedings, many of them make the transition to eating the pellet mush from a saucer. Others can eventually eat pellets that have simply been soaked and softened.

Basic Recipe for Moistened Pellets

> *Soak 2 rounded tbsp pellets in ¼ cup water*
> *Add 1 tbsp baby food and any supplements*

Though not pulverized, the mixture is softer than dry pellets and ensures more fluid intake for rabbits who can't drink adequately on their own. Feed the wet-pellet mixture two–three times a day in a small dish. Keep it spooned into a mound that can be lapped up by bunny.

Pellets, by necessity, become a more prominent part of the special-needs diet. The total diet, however, should be balanced as much as possible with hay and fresh vegetables. You can chop or grate the vegetables if bunny has chewing difficulties.

Photographs: upper left, Jim Stoneburner; lower right, Amy Bremers

Using either of the wet-pellet recipes in a special-, needs diet plan, daily amounts might look like this:

Table 6. *Daily Totals for Disabled Rabbits*

Wet pellets (from either recipe): ½–1 cup
Grass hay: Unlimited
Leafy greens: 3 medium handfuls
Fresh fruit: 2 tbsp

NUTRIENT-DENSE DIETS

The diet suggestions on this page are derived from Susan Smith's seminar lecture given at the Rabbit Center.[4] Though most often we are cautioned to keep bunny slim, there are circumstances in which weight gain is desirable. Bunnies need nutrient-dense diets in cases of geriatric weight loss, cancer, malnutrition/starvation, diabetes, and weight loss due to reduced mobility.

After loss of muscle mass, bunnies can be switched to alfalfa/clover hays to increase their protein intake. An additional consideration for older rabbits is that taste and smell are lost with advanced age. So it's best to be flexible in food choices for our senior bunnies. Offer strong flavors, such as applesauce, pureed carrot, banana, mint, and fennel.

Underweight rabbits can also be switched to higher calorie pellets. Extruded kibbles, such as Kaytee Rainbow Exact or Carefresh Complete, which are highly flavorful can be used to add calories needed for building weight in elderbuns.

To increase calories and nutrients in pellet-mush mixtures, you can double the amount of canned pumpkin or baby food in the recipe. Underweight bunnies still need plenty of fresh vegetables to stimulate activity.

RENAL FAILURE

In cases of renal failure, the goal is to reduce the nitrogen burden on the kidneys, while preventing muscle breakdown and maintaining body weight. Foods to avoid are banana, dried fruit, squash, and melon. Most other fresh veggies and fruit are safe.

Feeding bunnies in renal failure means reducing the protein intake (but never below the requirement) and increasing carbohydrate and fat calories to replace protein.

It's important for bunnies in renal failure to have regular monitoring of their serum electrolytes, calcium and phosphorus. Based on test results, other changes might include adjusting calcium intake, lowering salt and potassium, or adding vitamin D.

DIETARY CHANGES TO LOWER CALCIUM

Bunnies need some calcium for their bones, but some need less than others. If your vet recommends reducing your bunny's calcium intake, try:

Calcium-reduction measures

> *Switch to grass hays*
> *Switch to timothy-based pellets*
> *Reduce to ½ serving pellets daily*
> *Increase veggie servings*
> *Use a crock/bowl to stimulate water intake*
> *Treat for bladder infections*

Which veggies are lowest in calcium? You can check Kathleen Wilsbach's list[5] of calcium content in vegetables most commonly given to rabbits ■

Syringe feeding *of pellet-mush slurry is the best answer for those who are unable to eat from a dish or have chewing problems.*

---

4. Susan Smith, "Rabbit Nutrition." Master Seminar 3 (2010). DVD: See page 94

5. Kathleen Wilsbach, "Lowering Blood Calcium," *House Rabbit Journal* III, no. 5 (1995) http://rabbit.org/lowering-blood-calcium/

Obesity in Rabbits—*Loving Thumper to Death*   By Susan Smith, PhD

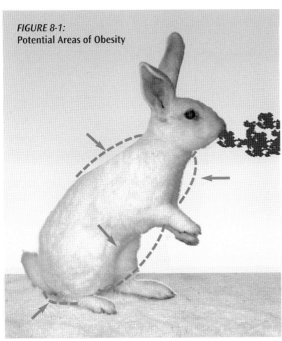

FIGURE 8-1:
Potential Areas of Obesity

Photograph your bunny's profile at a slim young age and compare it over the years. Fat may accumulate in the outlined areas.

SO YOU'VE FED THUMPER too many treat foods and unlimited pellets, and now your vet tells you that she's overweight. What do you do? Just as in humans, maintaining an ideal body weight is essential for your rabbit's good health. Obese rabbits find it difficult to reach their cecal pellets and clean themselves. Obesity places a heavy burden on the heart, can reduce cecum functions, and promotes diabetes and liver disease. In a medical emergency, excess body fat makes it difficult to predict your rabbit's response to anesthesia. Obesity turns a routine surgery into a high-risk event.

It's easy for excess weight to sneak up. I recommend taking a photograph of your rabbit's side profile, and then compare it over the years. A healthy weight profile resembles the slim silhouette, whereas an overweight rabbit looks more like the dashed outlines. If in doubt, ask your vet, and be brave enough to accept her honest answer.

Just like people, rabbits should lose fat weight slowly and safely. That is, no more than 1-2% of their body weight should be lost per week. This means, for example, that it should take two and one half to five months (10 to 20 weeks) for five-pound Thumper to lose that extra pound. This slower weight reduction helps your rabbit to readjust her metabolism to this new diet. Exercise is critical for weight reduction as well.

How do you implement this new diet? First, switch to a grass-based rather than an alfalfa-based pellet, because these have a lower caloric density. If not available in your area, ask your pet food store to stock it, or order directly on the Internet. Be sure to mix the new and old pellets initially, and reduce the volume gradually, so your rabbit has time to adjust. Use a measuring cup when dispensing pellets and follow the feeding guidelines. Offer unlimited grass hay so that Thumper has something to snack on between meals. Add fresh vegetables to the daily diet, and add new ones individually so her gut adjusts to these changes. Use fresh vegetables as a treat, instead of sugary or starchy foods. Carefully monitor your rabbit's weight and keep a written record of it.

By giving Thumper time to adjust to her new diet, both she and you will be rewarded with good health and a more active companion.   ∎

Susan Smith, PhD. *is Professor, Department of Nutritional Sciences, University of Wisconsin-Madison, with a Ph.D. in Biochemistry.*

Classes of Toxic Plants

By George Flentke, PhD

NOT ALL SPECIES or varieties of these plants has the same levels of toxins. Classification is based on the most dangerous plant of that species or variety.

An example is the Avocado. Avocados are of several varieties, only one of which contains toxins at dangerous levels to species other than humans.

Hybridization of the varieties for agricultural reasons has made it difficult to determine if the toxic variety is part of a hybrid species. Thus all avocados are assumed to be problematic.

Many plants are safe if treated to destroy toxins. Fruit trees are all listed as Class 1 toxins, but if the bark and branches are totally dried out, the toxins are destroyed. The sticks make wonderful rabbit chew toys. Remember if the sticks have any green in the bark (scrape through with a fingernail), then they are not dried. The seeds of all stone fruits (those with pits), apples and pears should be treated as Class 1 toxins even if dried.

Class 1: Universal species toxins, these are usually systemic toxins or local effect toxins of sufficient intensity to cause systemic problems. In general these plants should not be part of your household or they should be well protected from rabbits. *(continued)*

CLASS ONE					
Anenome	California Holly	False parsley	Jimson Weed/	Orange Sneezeweed	Sheep Laurel
Angel's Trumpet	Carolina jasmine	False Wild grape	Thorn Apple	Paradise Plant	Silverleaf nightshade
Apple	Castor Bean	Flowering maple	Jonquil	Peach Tree	Sneezeweed
Apricot	Chalice Vine	Flypoison	Karela	Pear Tree	Spider Climbing Lilly
Arrowgrass	Cherry Laurel	Fool's Parsley	Laburnum	Perill mint	Spotted Dumb Cane
Autumn Crocus	Chinese bellflower	Foxglove	Lambkill	Periwinkle	Squill
Avocado	Chinese Lantern	Fruit pits	Larkspur	Peyote	Stinkweed
Azalea	Chokecherry	Glory Lilly	Leucaena	Pheasant's Eye	Swamp Laurel/
Baby Wood Rose	Christmas Berry	Gold Dieffenbachia	Ligustrum	Plum Tree	Bog Laurel
Balsam Apple	Christmas Rose	Goldenchain	Lillies	poison Ash	Sweetheart Ivy
Balsam Pear	Cocklebur	Goldenrain	Lily-of-the-Valley	poison Hemlock	Tansy
Baneberry (white, red,	Coyotillo	Greasewood	Lobelia	poison ivy	Toadstools
black)	Crowpoison	Halogeton	Lupines	Poison nut	Tomato
Beefsteak plant	Daffodil	Hawaiian Baby Wood	Mandrake	Poison Oak	Toyon
Bittersweet	Daphne	Rose	May Apple	Poison sumac	Trumpet Flower
Bitterweed	Day-Blooming Jessamine	Hellebore	Meadow saffron	Poke salad	Trumpet Plant
Black Cherry	Deadly Nightshade	Henbane	Mescal	Pokeweed	Tullidora
Black Nightshade	Death Camas	Horse Nettle	Milk Vetch	Poppy	Variable Dieffenbachia
Bladderpod	Delphinium	Indian Hemp	Milkweed	Potato	Water Hemlock
Bloodroot	Devil's Tomato	Indian tobacco	Molds in Hay	Precatory bean	Water Parsnip
Blue Gum	Dieffenbachia	Indigo	Monkshood	Prickly poppy	Wild Carrot
Bluebonnet	Doll's eyes	Inkberry	Moonflower	Privet Hedge	Wild cucumber
Boxwood	Dumbcane	Inkweed/	Moonseed	Purple Mint	Wild Jessamine
Buddhist Pine	Elderberry	Drymary	Morning Glory	Red Sage	Wild mushrooms
Bunchberry	English Ivy	Jasmine	Mother-in-Law Plant	Rhododendron	Wild Peas
Buttercup/ Ranuncula	English Laurel	Jequirity Beans	Mountain Laurel	Ripple Ivy	Windflower
Butterfly Weed	Eucalyptus	Jerusalem Cherry	Mushrooms	Rosary pea	Wolfsbane
Calico bush/ Mountain	European Nightshade	Jessamine	Needlepoint Ivy	Rosebay	Wood-rose
Laurel	Exotica	Jimmy Fern/	Nutmeg	Rose-bay	Yellow jasmine
	perfection	Cloak Fern	Oleander	Scilla	Yew

"Check all plants to make sure that chewing is confined only to that suspected plant."

Class 2: Local toxins, allergens, dermal-sensitivity toxins or systemic toxins of lesser strengths. Since rabbits inevitably chew items, these toxins could be more of a problem than the current literature indicates. View these plants with caution.

Class 3: Low risk plants. Low-level toxins or toxins that herbivores, such as rabbits, routinely handle better than non-herbivore species. This class also contains plants that have historically been considered quite toxic, but recently whose toxicity is being re-evaluated as nontoxic or low toxicity.

FOR SUSPECTED POISONING

Call your vet. Bring in the whole suspected plant or chewed parts of the plant. Check all plants to make sure that chewing is confined only to that suspected plant.

Class 1: Call your vet immediately or go to an emergency clinic.

Class 2: Call your vet for consultation on whether an appointment is warranted.

Class 3: Watch rabbit carefully for any signs of poisoning or ill health. Call your vet if you feel it is warranted. ◼

| **George Flentke, PhD.** *is a biochemist at the University of Wisconsin-Madison and also Chapter Manager of House Rabbit Society's Madison chapter.*

Toxicity Classes © 2005, 2013 by George Flentke. All rights reserved. Used by kind permission.

CLASS 2

African Blue Lilly
Agapanthus
Alder Buckthorn
Amaryllis
American Hellebore
Anthurium
Arrowhead vine
Barberry
Bear Grass
Begonia (sand)
Bird of Paradise
Bleeding Heart
Blue Gum
Bracken Fern
Buckeye/Horse Chestnut
Buckthorn
Burning Bush
Butternut
Cactus
Caladium
Calendula/Pot Marigold
Calla Lilly
Candelabra Cactus
Cardinal Flower
Carnations
Cassine
Century Plant
Ceriman/Split-Leaf Philodendron/ Mexican Breadfruit
Chinaberry Tree
Chinese Inkberry
Clematis
Climbing Bittersweet
Coffee Bean/ Senna Bean
Coral Berry/ Snowberry

Cordatum/ Philodendron
Corn Cockle
Corn Plant
Cow Parsnip
Cowslip
Crinum Lily
Croton
Crown of Thorns
Crown Vetch
Cut-leaf Philodendron
Cycads
Cyclamen
Dasheen
Dessert Tobacco
Devil's Ivy
Dianthus
Dracaena palm/ Ribbon Plant
Dutchman's Breeches
Dutchman's Pipe
Elephant Ear
Emerald Feather
Emerald Fern
Eucalyptus
Euonymus
Everlasting Pea
Eyebane
False Hellebore
False Sago Palm
Fern Palms
Fiddleneck
Fireweed
Fishtail Palm
Florida Beauty
Fruit Salad Plant
Geranium (California)
Gladiola
Gold Dust Dracaena
Golden Pothos
Green Cestrum
Green gold Nephthysis
Guajillo

Hogweed
Hogwort
Horsebrush
Horsetail Reed
Hunter's robe
Hyacinth
Hydrangea
Indian Poke
Indian Tobacco
Inkberry
Iris
Jack-in-the-Pulpit
Japanese Pagoda Tree
Locoweed
Lucky Bamboo
Madagascar Dragon Tree/Red-Margined Dracaena
Marble Queen
Marijuana
Marsh Marigold
Meadow Pea
Mesquite
Mexican Breadfruit
Miniature Croton
Mistletoe
Nephthytis/ Chinese Evergreen
Night Jessamine
Oak Tree
Panda
Paper-flowers
Partridge Breast
Peace Lilly
Pencil Tree
Peony
Persian Violet Philodendron
Pigweed
Pingue/Colorado Rubber weed
Plumosa Fern

Poinciana
Pot Mum/Spider Mum
Pothos
Prickly copper-weed
Pride of Barbados
Rabbitbrush
Rayless golden-rod
Red princess
Rhubarb
Sacahuista
Saddle leaf Philodendron
Sago Palm
Sand Begonia
Satin Pothos
Schefflera
Scindapus
Shamrock Plant/Oxalis
Silver Pothos
Skunk Cabbage
Snow-on-the-mountain
Solomon's Seal
Spathe Flower
Split Leaf Philodendron
Star of Bethlehem
Strawberry Bush
Striped Dracaena
Sweet Flag
Sweet Pea
Swiss Cheese Plant
Tallow, Chinese/ Japanese
Tansy
Tara
Taro Vine
Tobacco
Tree Philodendron

Tulip
Umbrella plant
Variegated Philodendron
Variegated Rubber Plant
Walnut
Warneckei Dracaena
White Snakeroot
Wild Tobacco
Wisteria
Yaupon Holly

CLASS 3

Acacia
African Rue
Aloe Vera
Alsike Clover
Apple Leaf Croton
Asparagus Fern
Baccharis
Betel Nut Palm
Black Locust
Black Root/Black Snakeroot
Black Walnut
Blue Cohosh
Boston Ivy
Broomweed
Calamondin Orange Tree
Cineraria/ Groundsel
Creeping Charlie (not house-plant)
Cuban Laurel
Daisy
Emerald Duke
Fiddle-leaf Fig
Firecracker
Firethorn
Fireweed
Four O'clock
Gentians
German Ivy

Gill over the Ground
Ginko
Goatweed
Ground Ivy
Groundsel
Heart Ivy
Heartleaf
Holly Tree/Bush
Horse-Head
Indian Laurel
Indian Rubber plant
Johnson Grass
Juniper
Kafir
Klamath Weed
Lechiguilla
Maiden Hair Tree
Majesty
Medicine Plant
Milo
Poinsettia
Primrose
Purple Sesbane
Pyracantha
Rattlebox
Rattleweed
Red Emerald
Silverling
Snakeweed
Sorghum
Sprengeri Fern (asparagus)
St. Johns Wort
String of Beads
String of Pearls
Sudan grass
True Aloe
Turpentine Plant
Virginia Creeper
Weeping Fig
Wild Cucumber/ Balsam Apple
Wild Pea
Woodbine
Yerba-de-pasmo

Chapter Nine

Rabbit Medicine

Fortunately for today's bunnies, advanced medical treatment is available to them that we did not believe possible in the past.

WIDESPREAD INTEREST IN RABBITS as companions has brought about significant changes in their treatment. "Rabbit Veterinary medicine has progressed dramatically compared to twenty years ago when most of the knowledge was based on laboratory medicine of rabbits which is very limited compared to rabbits as companions."[1]

When House Rabbit Society held its Rabbit Veterinary Conference in 1997, it was the first and only conference that focused entirely on the treatment of rabbits. Our plan for another conference in about five years became unnecessary, because increased demand for better rabbit care forced rabbit medicine onto the agenda of nearly every small-animal conference in the world.

1. Debra Scheenstra, "New Developments in Rabbit Medicine and Care." Rabbit Center lecture (2012).

The Physical Design: *Some things we need to know*

BECOMING FAMILIAR with rabbits' physical functions and reading what their bodies tell us, we can employ preventive care. Being aware of their fragile skeletons, we learn proper handling and avoid broken bones. Knowing that bunnies protect their bones with strong muscles, we allow them sufficient muscle-building exercise. By understanding what happens in their gastro-intestinal tract, we avoid many problems and enable our bunnies to maintain healthy digestion.

***In fine form** (above), Moki poses for an adoption photo, showing off good body tone and posture.*
***Tree bark** (below) attracts domestic rabbits, as well as their wild cousins.*

In looking at a rabbit's torso (page 68), you will see the enormous amount of space that is allocated to digestive function. The previous chapter dealt with what to feed your rabbit for nutrition. This section explains how that food is processed.

DIGESTIVE PROCESSING

The way rabbits digest their food is truly amazing. Though rabbits churn food in their stomach the same way as other animals, their intestines handle it quite differently.

The small intestine, which is very long in a rabbit, absorbs sugars, starches, protein, and most nutrients. Dietary fiber keeps material flowing through the small intestine to the cecum and colon, where it is processed according to size.

The cecum is the large fermenting vat filled with beneficial food-digesting bacteria and protozoa. It produces volatile fatty acids, which are absorbed directly into the bloodstream. The cecum pushes out large particles, while retaining small cellulose particles, along with excess sugar, starch, and protein from the small intestine. A portion of the cecal contents is emptied daily. The cecum empties at a slower rate when dietary fiber is low.[2]

The colon, or large intestine, does some unique things in rabbits. In addition to forming fecal pellets, it separates small particles and sends them backwards into the cecum. Large fiber particles are sent on their way from here for a quick passage through the colon to become the large hard marbles that you see in your bunny's litterbox.

RECYCLING PLAN

At times, wild rabbits must rely on twigs and shrubs that are nutritionally low quality for other animals. They survive by consuming a large volume and converting it to higher quality protein and energy. The cecum does this job by producing B-complex vitamins and protein to be reingested. The vitamin/protein-rich material from the cecum is packaged into little clusters of cecotropes, which are an important part of your bunny's diet. They are enclosed in a mucus-membrane coating, which protects cecotrope bacteria from stomach acid, allowing them to ferment several more hours in the stomach after they are reingested. Finally the cecotropes are ready to pass to the small intestine where the nutrients are absorbed.

That's a pretty elaborate, round-about way of getting nourishment out of a blade of grass or the

2. E.Sakaguchi, "Digesta retention and fibre digestion in brushtail possums, ringtail possums and rabbits." *Comparative Biochemistry and Physiology* 96A :351(1990)

Photograph: upper, Ken Mark

oak-tree bark (or your baseboard) that your bunny has been nibbling on, but it works for wild rabbits who must get the most out of the poor food sources that are available. Nature has designed for them this complicated plan of food processing and reprocessing to get maximum nutrients. Domestic rabbits, with the same physical design and much richer diets, can easily gain excessive weight.

DIGESTIVE DISORDERS

The rabbit GI (gastrointestinal) tract depends on dietary fiber to keep everything moving at full speed. When motility slows down or stops, the result can be life threatening. Most motility problems can be prevented by plenty of hay. But sometimes rabbits don't consume the necessary fiber, because of stress, dental disorders, or other diseases, so it's important to correct any underlying problems.

The old diagnosis of "hairball" was used to describe accumulation of hair in the stomach. This is currently NOT thought to be a disease condition in itself. It becomes a problem only when motility stops, and the hair doesn't pass. The *House Rabbit Journal* archive covers more in-depth reading on these disorders.[3]

Upper GI impactions and bloat. Sometimes a small dense plug of hair can get through the stomach and lodge in a narrow passage in the small intestine, usually at the duodenum. The resulting obstruction stops the flow from the stomach.

Bloat is a serious condition that may develop secondary to impaction anywhere in the GI tract.

3. Susan Brown, "Sluggish Motility in the Gastro-intestinal Tract," *House Rabbit Journal* III, no. 7 (1996)
    http://rabbit.org/sluggish-motility-in-the-gastrointestinal-tract-2/

Diagram: Bob Harriman

FIGURE 9.1: Rabbit Gastrointestinal Tract

Esophagus. Swallowed plant food is passed through to the *stomach*

Stomach. Muscular contractions churn the food in a circular path, mixing them with the *gastric fluid*.

Small Intestine (comprised of the *duodenum, jejunum*, and *ileum*). The major part of digestion takes place in the small intestine. Some sugars, most starches, and up to 90% of all protein are absorbed.

Ileocecocolonic junction. Material is separated into large and small particles. Larger particles are sent to the colon for elimination. Smaller particles are sent to the *cecum* for fermentation.

Cecum (fermenting vat). Bacteria digest small-fiber cellulose, along with remaining protein, sugars, and starches that haven't been digested in the small intestine. B-complex vitamins and volatile fatty acids are produced and absorbed directly into the bloodstream.

Colon/Large Intestine. Contractions of the *haustrae* (circular muscle fibers in the *proximal colon*) further separate small particles, sending them backward into the cecum. Undigested fiber and waste (hard *fecal pellets*), along with fermented cecal material (*cecotropes*), pass through the *distal colon*.

Anus. Fecal pellets are eliminated. Cecotropes, packaged in mucus-membrane clusters, are consumed directly and returned to the digestive system.

ESOPHAGUS

PYLORIC VALVE *(small intestine begins)*

LIVER

Reingested cecotropes *continue to ferment, in the stomach, for several hours before passing to the small intestine for absorption*

STOMACH

PANCREAS

DUODENUM

SMALL INTESTINE

JEJUNUM

PROXIMAL COLON

APPENDIX

HAUSTRAE

Ileocecocolonic junction

ILEUM

CECUM

Fermenting cecal material

DISTAL COLON

RECTUM

ANUS

Sources: McLaughlin, C.A. and R.B. Chaisson, *Laboratory Anatomy of the Rabbit* (1990): 59-64; Percy, D.H. and S.W. Barthold. *Pathology of Laboratory Rodents and Rabbits* (1993):179-80

"If these harmful bacteria continue to grow, they can produce deadly toxins..."

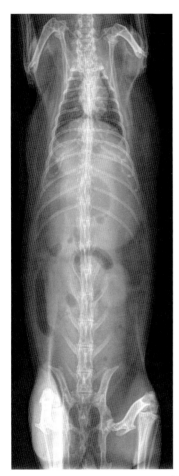

Stasis episode: *Buster's x-ray diagnosis was "large, fluid-filled stomach with gas bubble." A secondary problem was azotemia. He fully recovered from both problems with treatment.*

Gas can form directly behind a blockage or in any area where motility has slowed down, extending the stomach or the part of the intestine affected. Bloat can cause severe discomfort, shock, and death if not treated. In many cases, bloat occurs in the stomach itself, where immediate relief can be achieved with a gastric tube to remove gas. Treatment also includes pain medication and intravenous fluids to rehydrate and soften the impaction.

Altered gut flora. A rabbit relies on anaerobic bacteria (grown without oxygen) in the cecum to break down cellulose. If the microbial balance of the cecum is altered, an overgrowth of harmful bacteria may result that can make your bunny sick. And not only that—if these harmful bacteria continue to grow, they can produce deadly toxins that can kill your rabbit (enterotoxemia). Altered gut flora can be caused by moldy food, an overload of sugar or starch, or certain oral antibiotics. This is why veterinarians can prescribe only drugs for rabbits that work on the illness without destroying necessary digestive bacteria.

Enteritis (inflammation of the small intestine) can occur in rabbits when the cecum has slowed down enough to alter the gut flora. This affects the area of the small intestine (the ileum) next to the cecum. The intestinal lining produces a mucus coating over the inflamed area.

Cecal impaction occurs when more low-fiber material enters the cecum than exits. Since the cecum empties at a slower rate when fiber intake is low, impaction is less likely on a high fiber diet.

Another cause of cecal impaction is dehydration. This may be due to hot weather or insufficient water intake. When fluids are needed elsewhere in the body, they are drawn from the cecum's reservoir into the blood, leaving a hard accumulating mass in the cecum.

Any of the above conditions is usually accompanied by obvious pain, shown in bunny's posture. Bunny will not want to eat or drink, thus contributing to the severity of the problem.

An excellent article can be read online for more detail on these conditions and treatment.[4]

LITTERBOX INDICATORS

Your bunny's digestion can be monitored via the litterbox. You should see healthy piles of regular dry round marbles. But sometimes you might see these abnormalities:

Small scanty droppings indicate that less is coming through the GI tract. Eating less? GI Slowdown?

Marbles in ropes of hair mean a lot of hair is being swallowed. This is not a problem, as long as the hair is passing. Brushing removes loose hair and reduces the amount bunny swallows.

Excessive amount of cecotropes left unconsumed in soft clusters may mean that the diet is too rich in protein or that the bunny can't reach them.

Watery diarrhea means that digestion has shut down. Contact your vet right away. ∎

4. Dana Krempels, Mary Cotter and Gil Stanzione, "Illeus in Domestic Rabbits," *Exotic DVM* 2, no.4 (2000) http://www.bio.miami.edu/hare/ileus.html

Diagnostics: *Tests commonly used*

MANY RABBIT DISEASES are caused by pathogens (harmful microbes) that enter your rabbit's body in various ways. Air-born pathogens can be inhaled into the respiratory tract. Some might ascend up the urinary tract. Others may enter through wounds to the skin And still others are swallowed in contaminated food or water.

Some rabbit diseases are secondary to other problems, sometimes congenital, and sometimes developing over a period of time with no known cause. Fortunately, there are many diagnostic tools available to your veterinarian. Together with the veterinary assessment, diagnostic tests help determine the diagnosis and treatment.

The following descriptions were extracted from much more comprehensive material presented by Dawn Sailer at the Rabbit Center.[5]

IMAGING

Radiographs identify major organ changes/displacements, focusing on differences in opacity. Heart disease can sometimes be detected by radiographs but more definitively with ultrasound.

Ultrasound (sound waves bouncing off organs) provides additional detail not seen on x-ray and is most useful at revealing heart, liver, kidney disease, and sometimes cysts or abscesses within the thorax.

MRIs and CT scans (magnetic resonance imaging and computed tomography) are good for looking at bone and internal tissues and provide detailed radiographic pictures.

ECG/EKG (electrocardiogram) is done to assess heart problems.

LABORATORY WORK

Urinalysis will provide value levels for pH, specific gravity, blood, glucose, protein, and turbidity.

CBC and blood chemistry (complete blood count and general chemistry panel) can detect liver and kidney disease.

Fecal Float can show the presence or absence, in that particular sample, of intestinal parasites, such as pinworms, coccidia, and giardia. Analysis requires laboratory experience, as rabbit parasites look different than dog/cat parasites.

Culture and Sensitivity tests take five to seven days to get results. These are used to identify bacteria infecting a rabbit. In addition to fighting invaders from the outside, rabbits can also become infected by opportunistic bacteria already residing within their GI tract or on their skin surface. These bacteria are not normally a problem unless they are introduced to sterile areas of the body, i.e. blood or subcutaneous tissue. This happens when skin or membrane barriers are penetrated by a puncture or a bite wound, allowing entry of surface bacteria. The infection may remain in the local area, or it may become septicemic and spread via the blood from a less critical location to a vital organ.

Samples of tissue or pus from an infected area can be sent by your vet to a laboratory for identification of the infecting agents and a list of the drugs they are sensitive to. Your veterinarian uses this information in prescribing the appropriate drug.

Immunoassays test the immune response to a particular stimulus. We often use the ELISA (enzyme linked immunosorbant assay) for detecting an immune response to E. cuniculi, C. piliformis, and P. multocida. Positive results don't

---

5. Dawn Sailer-Fleeger, "Common Clinical Diagnostic Tests." Master Seminar 3 (2010). DVD: See page 94

Testing positive in 2006 to E.cuniculi, Jasmine lost her hop in 2011 but not her attitude. Her attentive partner, Dickens (seen tossing the red ball on page 38), remains free of any disease symptoms.

necessarily mean that the rabbit has an active infection but rather that he has been exposed to the pathogen and is producing antibodies to it.

WHAT TO EXPECT FROM POSITIVE RESULTS

Encephalitozoon cuniculi ((E. cuniculi) is a sporozoan parasite, usually passed in the urine of infected rabbit and ingested by another rabbit. While sometimes causing damage to the urinary tract, the parasites more often migrate to the brain, where they may cause neurological disorders. Many rabbits never show clinical signs of disease, and infection is only detected at necropsy as shown in the Rabbit Health Database table below.

TABLE 8-7. *Ratio of disease symptoms to seropositive rabbits*

ELISA TEST	SEROPOSITIVE RABBITS	DEVELOPED SYMPTOMS	POST MORTEM EVIDENCE FOUND
E.cuniculi	259	65	37
C.piliformis	120	9	28
P.multocida	50	3	incomplete

Clostridium piliformis is a spore-forming bacterium causing Tyzzer's disease, passing in fecal material from an infected animal. The disease may result in immediate illness—bloat/diarrhea/enteritis—and even death. The infection may enter the bloodstream and damage the liver and heart, leaving them predisposed to other diseases; and sometimes no disease is seen at all.

Pasteurella Multocida is a bacterium causing pasteurellosis, which is usually a disease of the upper respiratory tract but can also spread to inner ears, lacrimal ducts and lungs. Some rabbits harbor chronic infections in these areas but have negative nasal cultures. Measuring antibodies in serum is helpful in detecting infections in these rabbits.[6]

DRUG THERAPY

The purpose of testing is to provide your vet with enough information to prescribe appropriate treatment. Drug therapy might last several weeks, several months, or even a lifetime, depending on whether its treating chronic condition, such as heart disease or a persistent infection.

Since most drugs are developed for humans, we sometimes lose a good rabbit drug because of human complications. George Flentke's seminar lecture at the Rabbit Center explains why certain drugs work well in rabbits, while others don't. He tracks the evolution of the drugs through their second and third generation, showing how each one has improved or reduced its usefulness in rabbit medicine—particularly valuable information to rabbit caregivers.[7]

COMPLEMENTARY MEDICINE

Dr. Carolynn Harvey clarification is, "It's not a matter of choosing 'either, or'. It's a matter of expanding the range of treatment available."

Complementary medicines include chiropractic, acupuncture, massage, physical therapy, herbal, homeopathic, and food supplements. Specialists can work with your veterinarian in all of these areas. If you are interested in adjunctive therapies, Judith Pierce suggests starting with your veterinarian, who is familiar with your bunny's needs.[8] Your vet can make referrals and prescribe the therapies that might be beneficial.   ■

6. Barbara Deeb, "Pasteurella multocida Infection in Rabbits. http://rabbit.org/pasteurella-multocidainfection-in-rabbits/
7. George Flentke, "Rabbit Therapeutics: The good, the Bad & the Ugly." Master Seminar 3 (2010). DVD: see page 94.
8. Judith Pierce, "Alternative Therapies." Master Seminar 1 (2010). DVD: See page 94

Rabbit Formulary

By Carolynn Harvey, DVM

ANTIBIOTICS

Amikacin: 15 mg/kg SQ SID

Amoxicillin: *DO NOT USE*

Azithromycin (Zithromax): 20 mg/kg q24h initially, then 2x/week, or prn for maintenance. *Watch for GI upset.*

Cephalosporins: *DO NOT USE*

Chloramphenicol: 20-50 mg/kg BID PO *(have specially formulated)* or 20 mg/kg SQ BID *(stings, may need to dilute). Minimize your exposure. Wear gloves. Wash your hands after handling, and keep out of reach of children.*

Ciprofloxacin: 10-20 mg/kg PO SID

Enrofloxacin (Baytril): 5-10 mg/kg PO or SQ BID or 10- 20mg/kg SID (may see GI upset at 20 mg/kg). *Can be given IV, but give slowly and watch for histamine release.*

Doxycycline Hyclate: 2.5 mg/kg PO BID: A semisynthetic tetracycline that can be given with food and does not bind with calcium.

Marbofloxicin: 10 mg/kg, PO SID

Metronidazole: 10mg/kg PO BID

Pen G, Benzathine/Procaine: 20,000:30,000 u/# SQ every other day for 2-6 weeks, then same dose 2x/week. *Watch for GI upset, which can be fatal. In repeat uses, watch for anaphylaxis (consider dispensing epinephrine for emergency use).*

Pen G, Procaine: 20,000-30,000 u/# (0.05-0.1 cc/#) SQ daily for short periods, or once a week *(recommended by VIN)*

Trimethoprim-Sulfa: 30 mg/kg PO BID

NSAIDS, ANALGESICS

Aspirin: 40-80 mg/kg PO BID (empirical dose); 100mg/kg BID (published dose)

Buprenorphine: 0.005 : 0.01 mg/kg SQ, IM or in mouth. *Note that this is lower than the published dose, which seems too sedating . Is more effective when absorbed by the mouth than when swallowed.*

Butorphanol (Torbugesic): 0.25 mg/kg /SQ, IM, IV. Can be used orally, but short half life.

Carprofen: 1 mg/kg PO BID. Conservative dose, can probably safely double. *Watch for azotemia, rare "sedated" reaction.*

EMLA Cream: Shave area, apply cream, wait 5 minutes for superficial numbing. *Wear gloves to apply.*

Flunixin Meglumine (Banamine): 1 mg/kg SQ or IV

Ibuprofen: 7.5-20 mg/kg PO BID–TID

Children's Motrin: 20mg/cc *Watch for GI upset, typhlitis.*

Ketoprofen: 1 mg/kg SQ

Meloxicam: 0.2-0.5 mg/kg PO SID–BID. Dr Harvey's starting dose is 0.2 mg/kg BID. *HRS fosterers report that it doesn't seem to last 24 hours at 0.1 mg/kg for postop pain*

GI DRUGS

Cisapride: 2.5-5 mg per rabbit PO TID. *This is no longer on the market and needs to be obtained through a compounding pharmacy.*

Cholestyramine: 2g in 20 ml water PO SID

Metoclopramide (Reglan): 0.2-0.5 mg/kg PO, SQ, IV TID

Sucralfate: 125 : 250 mg per rabbit TID as slurry

Sulfadimethoxine (Albon): 25 mg/kg PO SID x 14 days, or until fecal is negative

PARASITICIDES

Albendazole: 7-20 mg/kg SID x 3-6 months for E. cuniculi

Carbaryl powder: 2x per week

Fenbendazole (Panacur): 20 mg/kg SID x 21 days for E. cuniculi

Fipronil (Frontline): *DO NOT USE (seizures and death reported)*

Imidacloprid (Advantage): Use cat dose

Ivermectin 1% (Ivomec): 300mcg/kg PO or SQ every 7-14 days

Lufenuron (Program): Use cat dose

Lime-Sulfur Dip (Lym Dip): Every one to two weeks. *Dipping/bathing process itself can cause shock or collapse.*

Oxibendazole: 20mg/kg SID x 3-6 months for E. cuniculi

Selamectin (Revolution): 6-12 mg/kg monthly (15 mg for rabbits under 4 lbs., 30 mg for rabbits over 4 lbs.)

Dr. Carolynn Harvey *practices veterinary medicine at Chabot Veterinary Clinic in Hayward, California. She is also Health Director at the Rabbit Center, in Richmond, California.*

Veterinary Care: *The primary means to health*

Exam day at HRS: Foster volunteers Judy Hardin (top) and Rich Sievers (2nd from top) cuddle with bunnies at the Rabbit Center, while waiting for appointments with Dr. Harvey (upper right).
To determine sex *apply pressure above the genital area (lower left and right). The protruded vulva is pointed, whereas the penis protrusion is round.*

ONE OF THE MOST IMPORTANT ALLIANCES you will ever form to ensure your rabbit's longevity is with your veterinarian. You must be able to work together on bunny's health care program. Find a good rabbit doctor[9] and make the first appointment as soon as possible.

PHYSICAL EXAM

Your veterinarian will start your bunny with a head-to-toe exam at the clinic, where the file will be set up. Then you will be ready if an emergency arises. Your bunny's weight and temperature will be recorded and compared to future exams. With new bunnies, it's advisable to recheck the gender. This is not so easy to do if your bunny is extremely young, because the genitals of immature males and females look similar.

Then the veterinarian will check for respiratory disease, listen to heart and digestive sounds, and palpate the abdomen to check for organ or intestinal abnormalities. During the palpation, the veterinarian will also check for lumps and bumps that may indicate bacterial infection or tumors.

Depending on your rabbit's age and health conditions, your veterinarian may recommend a blood panel to check for problems, such as anemia, renal failure, and elevated liver enzymes. In a pre-operative exam, blood work may also help indicate any special precautions that need to be taken prior to or during surgery. Routine blood work and radiographs are part of geriatric exams.

If your bunny is over five–six years old, a comprehensive physical exam is recommended every six–twelve months. Your bunny's ongoing health

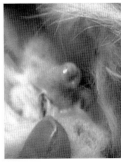

9. HRS Educators, "How to Find a Good Rabbit Vet." HRS website, http://rabbit.org/faq-how-to-find-a-good-rabbit-vet/

"New instruments have transformed the methods of monitoring patients during surgery."

relies on your veterinarian's knowledge and your own ability to follow through on prescribed plans.

SPAY/NEUTER

Neutering helps both health and behavior. Males can be neutered as soon as the testicles have descended. This can happen any time after three months. Females are usually spayed at six–eight months old, depending on size. In addition to preventing pregnancies, health benefits include fewer infections due to bites and scratches and less inclination to urinary infections. And a complete spay, of course, eliminates the risk of uterine cancer (up to 80% in five-year olds).

Our rabbits are not fasted like cats or dogs. However, their food is removed about an hour before surgery to prevent aspiration of leftover food in their mouth when they go under anesthesia. They are offered food as soon as they awaken.

ADVANCES IN SURGERY

Surgical equipment and techniques have improved in recent years, greatly reducing the risk of surgery-related deaths. Most veterinary hospitals are now equipped with isoflurane, which is the anesthesia of choice for rabbits. Safety of the procedure also depends on the skill of the practitioner, along with adequate preparations, pre-anesthetics, and monitoring techniques.

Halothane is used in many low-cost neuter clinics. Halothane can be used safely if precautions are taken. Since the combination of halothane and adrenaline can be lethal, rabbits should be well sedated with pre-anesthetic to reduce stress-induced adrenalin before halothane is administered.

New instruments have transformed the methods of monitoring patients during surgery. They are fairly standard in veterinary hospitals. Oxygen, carbon dioxide, EKG, temperature, and blood pressure are all tracked while bunny is under anesthesia, significantly improving survival rates.

RADIOLOGY ADVANCEMENTS

Most veterinary hospitals have invested in some of the expensive technology that developed in human medicine. Remember how long we used to wait at the veterinarian's office for an x-ray to be developed? Now with digital radiographs, we get an almost instant view, accelerating the speed of the diagnosis, which may at times be the difference in life and death. New technology further benefits diagnosing and treating many common problems.

Veterinarians have improved their ability to diagnose and treat dental disease through the use of digital skull x-rays and new evaluation techniques. Many easy-to-use dental instruments have been developed in the past ten years that make dental problems much more treatable.

KEEPING RECORDS

Every time your bunny sees the vet, you should get copy of the exam record and any test results. Keep everything in chronological order and add your own notes as well. If you ever have to rush to an emergency clinic during the night, your file may be the only health record available. Even when you don't go to emergency, your home notes may save your own veterinarian valuable time, and they are often clipped right into the hospital record.

My home health care files include date, time, bunny's temperature, what first-aid treatment was given and response. I am prone to forget what I've learned from my bunnies' previous episodes, and then I am grateful that I have kept their records. ∎

Pre-preps and preps: A surgery patient is calmed, and her eyes are soothingly treated prior to other pre-anesthesia preparations.

Problems: *Causes and treatment*

CERTAIN HEALTH INCIDENTS will occur over your bunny's lifetime. Some of them are minor, while others may be serious. Paying attention to all of them will ensure that nothing is missed, so you know when a vet visit is needed.

Animal attacks. If your rabbit has been attacked by a dog, raccoon, or any predatory animal, take him to the vet, even if you see no bite wounds. These are sometimes unobservable without a veterinary exam. Also, a bunny might experience shock that may not be apparent for several hours. Precautionary treatment for shock is advisable anytime a rabbit has been subjected to an attack.

Bladder sludge / stones. A suspected cause is excess dietary calcium and Vitamin-D, though urinary infection is often involved. Treatment usually includes fluid therapy and antibiotics.

If a small stone is present, it may pass *painfully*, but most stones have to be surgically removed.

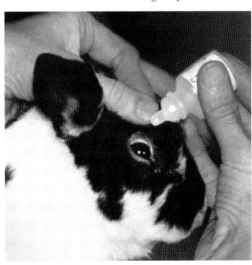

Runny-eye treatment: It's not always possible to find the cause or cure to runny eyes, but applying topical ophthalmic drops or ointment does seem to help relieve symptoms.

Bleeding toenails. When toenails grow too long, they can break off and bleed. This may not require rushing off to the vet, but it does require adequate cleaning with a disinfectant. You can apply styptic powder or cornstarch to stop the bleeding. Keep bunny confined on a clean surface until the bleeding has stopped. If bone is exposed, antibiotics might be required to prevent infection. Contact your veterinarian for treatment and prescription.

Broken bones. While many fractures show immediate symptoms (e.g., dragging one foot), others may not be so obvious. If the rabbit has suffered trauma and or is favoring one limb, X-rays are needed to determine the extent of the injury.

Conjunctivitis. Inflammation of the conjunctiva, or membrane lining the eyelids, may be caused by allergy or bacteria/viral infection, resulting in watery eyes. Sometimes nasal discharge occurs at the same time. Many rabbits with runny eyes show no other signs of illness.

Culturing for bacterial infection is sometimes difficult, so we normally treat topically, assuming there is one. Your veterinarian may choose to flush the tear ducts with saline solution and prescribe an ophthalmic ointment or drops.[10]

Cuts and lacerations allow surface bacteria to enter subdermal areas, often causing infection. Always have a bottle of wound disinfectant (poly-hydroxydine or chlorhexidine solution) on hand and use it immediately if bunny incurs a scratch. Follow up with triple-antibiotic ointment. Keep any cut, scratch, or laceration clean and check it daily for swelling. Deep cuts, punctures, or large

---

10. Dana Krempels, "Runny Eyes, Runny Nose. What Do They Mean?" http://www.bio.miami.edu/hare/sneezing.html.

wounds should be seen by the veterinarian, in case stitches and systemic antibiotics are necessary.

Dental disease. If your bunny is drooling or has chronic conjunctivitis, facial swelling, and seemingly decreased appetite, get a thorough dental exam even if the incisors look fine to you. There may be molar spurs, tooth root infections, or overgrown roots that penetrate the jawbone and, in some cases, may cause the narrowing of the nasolacrimal ducts.

Your veterinarian has the right instruments for filing overgrown incisors and molar spurs and extracting loose teeth. X-rays can detect tooth root problems. If infection is involved, surgery may be needed, along with antibiotics. More details are available in a presentation by Kristen Strobel[11] as well as an online article by Dana Krempels.[12]

Diarrhea, constipation, bloat. This usually indicates gastrointestinal disorder (see page 67). Accompanying behavior will help determine the immediacy of veterinary care. If bunny has diarrhea, low temperature and is listless, take warming action (page 80) and rush him to the hospital!

If he is constipated, bloated (tight belly), and sitting in a tense position, listen to his abdomen. Too much or too little gut sounds are danger signs. Contact your veterinarian right away, as your bunny most likely needs a same-day appointment.

Ear mites. Noticeable signs are head and ear shaking. Inspection of the ear reveals dark scabby material inside it. While it's possible to work liquid medication down into heavily infested ears, this can be extremely painful. Instead give systemic oral or injectable ivermectin in doses a week apart. Topical selamectin is used once a month or as

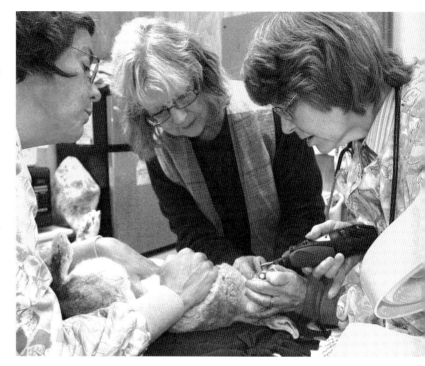

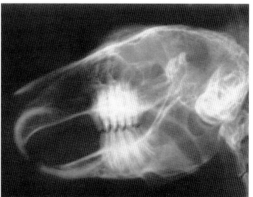

Tooth trim: *Volunteers (above) Karen Johanson and Terry Linscott assist Dr. Carolynn Harvey with a dremel trim on Buster's overgrown incisor.*
A healthy occlusion *looks like this (left). There are 28 teeth that continue to grow throughout a bunny's life. The opposing uppers and lowers grind against each other and keep the surfaces worn down. Maloccluded teeth that overgrow and prevent chewing/eating will need regular trimming.*

11. Kristen Strobel, "Dental Problems in Rabbits." Master Seminar 3 (2010). DVD: See page 94
12. Dana Krempels, "Dental Disease in Rabbits" http://www.bio.miami.edu/hare/dental.html.

Radiograph: courtesy Laura Wade, DVM, Clarence, NY

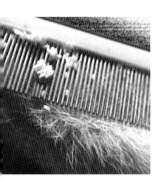

Fly eggs from the common house fly (upper) stick like little burrs in the coat. A daily flea combing can get rid of them before they hatch and do harm.
Itchy spine (lower) might indicate fleas or mites. Flaky dandruff can mean fur mites or flea allergy. You may see "flea dirt" that tells you fleas are present.

needed. Both eliminate mites on the bunny but not in the environment.

Flea infestation. Control of fleas is normally a matter of upkeep. Causing skin allergies in some rabbits, flea infestation also becomes a disease state when it is severe and masses of black grains of dirt (actually dried blood) are seen on the skin. Less agile animals who are not able to groom themselves can become anemic from blood loss incurred in prolonged flea infestation.

Attack the problem aggressively but not with a flea dip. For an already compromised animal, a dip can be fatal. And flea collars are lethal if chewed. Traditional (carbaryl) flea powders can be used, or a systemic treatment such as selamectin may be topically applied to the back of the neck (where bunny can't reach it). Products with imidacloprid or lufenuron have been safely used on rabbits. *Do not* use products containing fipronil.

Fly strike. Compromised animals are more vulnerable, but any rabbit with open wounds or a dirty bottom, may fall victim to egg-laying flies.

Maggots not only cause damage by burrowing into flesh, but they also release lethal toxins.

If you have cuterebra/botflies in your area and find suspicious "warble tumors," you need to see a vet for larvae removal.[13] For rabbits stricken by common houseflies, you can plunge the stricken area under running tap water and wash the maggots off yourself, but follow up with a vet visit. There may be more larvae or eggs that you have not detected, and your veterinarian can give IV/SQ fluids to detoxify and treat for shock.

Prevention is a must. Keep susceptible bunnies indoors with good screens on your doors and windows. If you can't keep flies off your bunny, you can prevent their damage by combing all eggs out of the fur on the hindquarters, feet, legs and tail.

Fur mites (cheyletiella). Evidence is seen especially on the lower spine where a thick layer of itchy flaky skin has developed. Often the clumps of hair will fall out along with the flakes of skin. Both flea allergies and fur mites cause these uncomfortable skin conditions. Both can be treated with flea powders. Again, use carbaryl powder (pyrethrins may cause respiratory problems. Fur mites, like ear mites, can be treated with ivermectin or selamectin.

Head tilt (torticollis) is often accompanied by flipping/rolling. The cause is usually a bacterial infection in the inner ear that affects the rabbit's balance. Other causes might be parasitic disease in the brain or a stroke. A veterinary exam is needed to diagnose the cause and prescribe treatment.

Heat stress. Bunny is panting and has a wet nose. Your freezer should have milk or juice cartons

13. Joy Gioia, "Fly Strike Emergency," *House Rabbit Journal* IV, no. 3 (2000), http://rabbit.org/fly-strike-emergency/

full of ice to put next to your bunny on hot days. Mist his ears with cool water and hang a wet towel across one end of the cage or pen. Then set up a fan for evaporative cooling.

Heart disease may be hidden behind other diseases. Bouts of enteritis are sometimes secondary to poor circulation caused by cardiovascular disease.[14] But whether the underlying cause of a GI problem is due to diet or to a heart condition must be determined by your vet. Usually a series of tests are needed before your veterinarian can diagnose heart disease and prescribe medication. Signs may be incoordination, weakness, weight loss, depression, enteritis, or difficult breathing.

Lumps, bumps. You needn't rush to the hospital in the middle of the night if you notice a lump on your normal-acting bunny. You should, however, make an appointment and have it checked fairly soon. Abscesses and tumors can be serious, and treatment depends on specifically what it is.

Paralysis. Partial or complete paralysis can have many diverse causes. Besides trauma to the head

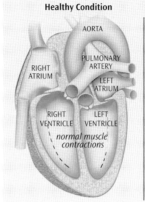

Figure 9.2: *Examples of a normal and a diseased rabbit heart*

Healthy Condition

AORTA
PULMONARY ARTERY
RIGHT ATRIUM
LEFT ATRIUM
RIGHT VENTRICLE
LEFT VENTRICLE
normal muscle contractions

Various Disease Conditions

Vein enlargement
Arterial calcification
Thromboembolism
Leaky valve
Flabby muscle *leading to: reduced muscle contraction; thin ventricle walls; scar tissue/ fatty deposits*
AORTA
PULMONARY ARTERY
RIGHT ATRIUM
LEFT ATRIUM
RIGHT VENTRICLE
LEFT VENTRICLE
Stiff muscle *leading to: small chamber; thick ventricle walls*

or back, causes may include strokes; tumors; bacterial or protozoan infections; viruses; nematodes; toxins; degenerative disease; congenital deformities and even osteoporosis and arthritis.

Rabbits who experience loss of mobility should have a complete neurological exam and blood workup. Treatment depends on the specific cause. For long-term home care see page 86.

Raccoon roundworm (Baylisascaris). Eggs are deposited in soil and vegetation where raccoons defecate and may be ingested by grazing animals. Since rabbits are not the target host, the larvae migrate to neural tissue causing nearly 100% mortality. No treatment is scientifically recognized, but some caregivers report success with parasitals.

Prevention is imperative. Keep all feed and hay securely stored, and keep bunny off the ground where raccoons have roamed.

Red urine. A urinalysis is needed to determine if there is blood in the urine. If blood is present, it may

Heart diseases *depicted in Figure 9.2 (above) are not all concurrent, but rather show examples of various disease conditions. When detected, many heart conditions can be treated.* **Paresis in rabbits** *(left): Bijou is the poster bunny for Amy Spintman's web pages on disabled-rabbit care (urls are listed on page 88). Paresis has a number of causes, but that number is surpassed with solutions for a happy existence.*

14. Barbara Deeb, "Cardiovascular Disease in Rabbits," *House Rabbit Journal* IV, no. 6 (2001), http://rabbit.org/cardiovascular-disease-in-rabbitsmore-questions-than-answers/

Photograph: Amy Spintman; heart diagram: Bob Harriman

Vet wrap protects Luke's feet (upper) where faultily healed broken legs left him predisposed to calluses. Moisture exposure from a runny eye (lower) caused Thaddeus to have skin inflammation and hair loss. The skin responded well to treatment with petrolatum ointment.

indicate infection, urinary stones, or possibly cancer. Otherwise the reddening of the urine color may be due simply to dietary or weather changes.

Respiratory disease. Noticeable symptoms are nasal discharge or sneezing. There may also be rattly or labored breathing, which in a rabbit is not short panting but rather long hard breaths.

Some rabbits may be experiencing allergic reactions to bedding material or simply to dust. The same symptoms may indicate a long-term chronic condition or the onset of a life-threatening disease.

Upper respiratory disease may be caused by infection or obstruction of the upper airways (nasal passages, sinuses, pharynx). Lower respiratory (lung) disease can be quite serious and may be caused by infection or tumors, or it might be secondary to heart disease. All respiratory diseases should be evaluated by a veterinarian to determine the course of treatment.

Sore hock/foot abscesses are perplexing problems not limited to heavy rabbits with feet on wire. The fur on any rabbit's feet can wear down, exposing the skin and forming calluses. Rabbits can run about on hardwood or linoleum floors without injury to their callused feet. It's the sitting surface that matters. It must be dry. That includes all resting boards. If the litterbox is not changed daily, keep it topped with dry material so that the surface next to the feet is always dry.

Moisture-damaged skin is easily cracked, allowing dirt to penetrate. Dirt in open foot-wounds nearly always causes difficult-to-treat infections. Disinfect all open wounds with polyhydroxydine or chlorhexidine solution, apply antibiotic ointment, and bandage the wounded area. If any swelling oc-

curs, take bunny to the veterinarian. Antibiotics and long-term treatment may be necessary.

Straining may indicate urinary problems if bunny postures to urinate but produces little urine. Sometimes a series of little puddles around the litterbox instead of in it and excessive water drinking are signs of urinary disease. Any of these symptoms warrant a veterinary exam.

Thymoma. This might be found when your bunny is being x-rayed for possible respiratory infection. A thymoma is a "benign" tumor that arises from the thymus gland and grows. While not a cancerous growth that metastasizes, it eventually causes death by squeezing the space in the chest cavity. Your veterinarian will monitor the growth.

If the growth is slow, your bunny may have a normal life expectancy; if rapid, your veterinarian may find a surgical expert to remove the thymoma or explore radiation and complimentary therapies, which have caused remission in several cases.

Urine scald may be an indication of urinary disease but more often is a secondary problem in crippled or arthritic rabbits who urinate on themselves. Skin constantly exposed to urine becomes inflamed. See "Skin Care," page 87 for treatment.

Wet cheeks are due to chronically runny eyes. Mild wetness can be blotted with tissue. If the eye discharge has already hardened and caked into the fur, clean with cotton swabs and warm water. Wait until it softens before gently combing out the remaining debris. If the fur in the path of the eye drainage is always wet, it may fall out and expose inflamed skin that resembles urine scald. The damaged skin can be treated with a moisturizing cream or ointment.. ∎

Chapter Ten

Home Care 10

Programs for home care involve feeding, exercising, grooming, and medicating the bunny, as well as cleaning the environment.

MOST OF YOUR BUNNY'S LIFE will be spent at home, where you provide essential care. If you have healthy bunnies, it will be simply a matter of proper feeding, exercise provisions and periodic grooming. If your bunny is convalescing after a serious illness, your veterinarian will set up a program to follow at home. If your bunny is chronically ill and will always need special care, your veterinarian's plan will be augmented by the techniques you develop for meeting your bunny's ongoing needs.

We all find housekeeping shortcuts so that our best time is spent where it really counts—directly with the bunnies, allowing us peaceful hours of grooming, petting, and watching.

On Watch: *The importance of being vigilant*

Taking temperature is one of the first things you should learn to do. If you are nervous, have your vet show you before you have an emergency. Unlike a cat or dog, a bunny is easier to check on her back. Use vaseline or other lubricant to coat the thermometer and slide it into the orifice that winks at you. Slide first over the pelvic bone, and then downward.

EVEN HEALTHY BUNNIES need to be monitored, though not as rigidly as those in delicate health. While it's impossible to have a remedy for every problem that could arise, appropriate treatment is available much sooner if you recognize when a problem does exist. Start with knowing your rabbit's normal behavior. Do a lot of watching and heed the clues.

Clue 1: Appetite. When we come around with the veggie basket in our house, we expect to see our bunnies standing up and begging for a treat. When one doesn't, we are alerted to a possible health problem. It doesn't always mean that we rush off to the vet, but it does mean that we place the bunny on watch until we investigate further. Is it just a fluke? Has he been eating a lot of hay and is just not hungry right now?

Clue 2: Accompanying behavior. In addition to not eating, what is the bunny's attitude? Does she seem listless? Where is she choosing to sit? What is her posture? Is she in a scrunched position, with ears pulled tightly together, or her eyes bulging? Is she crunching her teeth, squealing or whimpering?

None of this behavior was present when I found Dickens and Jasmine's pellet bowl nearly full. They normally leave it empty. I assumed Jasmine wasn't eating due to her history of jaw abscess. I felt her jaw (no swelling), and then her belly. It seemed full but soft and not bloated. I took her temperature. It was normal. She was stretched out in a comfortable position, not hunched up in misery. She looked bright and perky. It didn't make

sense—until I later discovered that I had switched pellet bowls. Jasmine and Dickens had eaten their normal ration from a bowl that was intended for a group of four. The lesson here is to include behavior when gathering your facts.

EVALUATING URGENCY

When bunny's appetite and behavior are off, the first thing to do is take her temperature. Is it below 100 or above 105? If it's low, take immediate warming action, e.g. heating pad, disc warmer, or a towel-wrapped hot water bottle (monitor for overheating). Start massaging the ears to warm them. "Medications and other treatment will not work properly if body temperature is too low. The first critical step is to get temperature up to normal."[1]

If the temperature is high, start cooling by dampening her ears with alcohol or cold water. You can also place ice packs on her abdomen. These are stopgap measures until you can get instructions from your veterinarian.

If your regular vet is unavailable, go to an emergency clinic for any of the following urgent conditions: painful, tight abdomen; watery diarrhea; respiratory distress (labored or open-mouth breathing); deep wounds, trauma, or broken bones (limb sticking out to the side or being dragged); or fly strike over a large area (see page 76).

If your bunny has a sudden head tilt or is rolling, keep her in a padded environment until she can be seen at your daytime veterinary clinic. Though not usually a life-threatening emergency, a veterinary exam is needed to diagnose the cause and prescribe treatment.   ■

---

1. Dana Krempels, "Emergency! What to do until you can get your bunny to the vet." Master Seminar 1 (2010). DVD: See page 94.

Convalescent and Chronic Care: *Managing medicine at home*

Whisky WHEN YOUR BUNNY COMES HOME to convalesce from surgery or a serious illness or injury after a hospital stay, recovery is expected. Your job is to provide the support and home care that your veterinarian prescribes.

AFTER STASIS RECOVERY

Bunnies who have suffered any of the gastrointestinal conditions described on page 67 are usually hospitalized until they are stable enough to return home for continuing treatment as follows:

Fluids are given subcutaneously (under the skin). Your veterinarian will show you how.

Motility drugs such as metoclopramide or cisapride (if available) help get the GI tract working.

Pain medication is usually prescribed to make bunny more comfortable and speed recovery.

Hay: Give any kind the rabbit will eat.

Leafy greens: Offer them several times a day

Encourage fiber intake by your anorexic bunny with constant fresh offerings. Until he is eating on his own, you may need to syringe feed one of the formulas on page 60.

Once your bunny's appetite has recovered, he should be watched carefully. Anorexia is both a sign of illness and a cause of further illness by slowing down GI motility all the more.

POST SURGERY/TRAUMA

Your bunny should be confined for a few days after spay/neuter surgery (about 2 days for males; 5-6 for females) in a clean disinfected cage or a small covered pen. Mixed sexes should be separated for about two weeks. Provide comfortable bedding and watch the suture area for signs of infection.

Confinement might be more restrictive for a much longer period of time for a bunny convalescing from fractures or back injuries. Rotate bunny's position on comfortable bedding to prevent bed sores and provide lots of toys to alleviate boredom.

Most bunnies are able to eat immediately after surgery, but some may be anorexic for a couple of days. Hay is especially good to feed at this time to get the digestive system working again. If your veterinarian advises supplemental syringe feeding, see page 64. After a hospital stay, your bunny will most likely have medication and treatment prescribed that will continue at home.

APPLYING TOPICAL MEDICATIONS

Home caregivers don't require a special skill to apply topical medications such as antibiotic ointment for wounds; dermal antibiotic/antifungal drops for infected skin areas; ivermectin for flea/mite infestations; otic drops for ear wax; or ophthalmic ointments/drops for conjunctivitis.

If your bunny has nasal congestion, your vet may instruct you to use a nebulizer.

INJECTABLE MEDICATIONS

Though a few drugs, such as certain pain medications, must be given in the muscle, most of the injections that you will be giving will be under the loose skin over the shoulders. Either way your vet will give you a demonstration on how it's done.

In some cases, a convalescing rabbit needs subcutaneous fluids, not only to keep up hydration but to balance electrolytes and help flush out toxins. Lactated Ringer's Solution (LRS) is given for a number of conditions including toxicity, kidney malfunction, fever, and digestive upsets. Sometimes B-vitamins are added to the bag of LRS to increase appetite for anorexic rabbits.

Home-care tips *are given to new adopters on a regular basis by Carolyn Mosher at the Rabbit Center.*

Photograph: Ken Mark

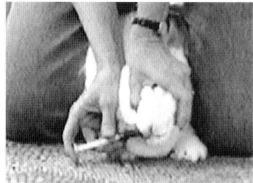

Missing teeth result in Jasmine's preference for a front approach (above). *Side insertion* (above right) is the usual access point. *Plunging position* from the palm of your hand (below) gives better control advises Joy Gioia of St. Louis HRS.

ORAL MEDICATIONS

By far the easiest way to give an oral medication is to have it in a tasty suspension that your bunny takes willingly, sometimes yanking the syringe right out of your hand.

If you must use persuasion, you will need to hold the bunny securely in an upright position while you insert the syringe—behind her incisors and in front of her molars. The x-ray on page 75 shows the gap between the incisors and molars.

Positions for caregivers: For many years, my preferred position was to kneel over the rabbit from behind with bunny trapped between my knees, inserting the syringe from the side (shown above). This was assuming the bunny was on the floor. More often you are leaning over a counter, where you have your bunny encircled in your arms.

Inserting the syringe: With one hand on the top of the head, (a) use your thumb to part the lips on the side, inserting the syringe with the other hand or (b) as Joy Gioia suggests, spread two fingers over the bridge of the nose forming an inverted "V" and guiding the syringe into the side of the mouth.[2]

For giving tablets, try the easy method first. Cut the pill into smaller chunks, which can be inserted into a couple of raisins, dried cranberries, or a slice of banana. If your bunny is particularly adept at removing the pills from the fruit, the chunks can be crushed into a powder and dropped into a 10-ml syringe with mashed banana or applesauce. Smaller syringes are tedious to load.

You can also mix the whole crushed tablet with juice or water, in which case you will need to do some math to figure out the strength of the liquid and the amount to draw into the syringe. I prefer the viscosity of a puree to a clear liquid. The thicker consistency is easier for my elderbuns to swallow, and there are fewer incidents of gagging/coughing.

STOCKING THE MEDICINE CABINET

As you acquire medicines from your veterinarian, they will be specific to the illness being treated. Some medications can be kept for recurring illness, as per your veterinarian's instructions. Check expiration dates, protect medications from contamination, and keep tools and bandages sterile. At the same time that you stock your bunny's medicine cabinet with specific medications, here are some general items to have on hand:

Alcohol	Plastic thermometer
Gauze bandages	Shaver/clippers
Heating pad/disc	Triple-antibiotic ointment
Oral syringes	Vet-wrap
Nebulizer	Vinyl gloves
Petroleum jelly	Wound cleanser ■

2. Joy Gioia, "Medicating and Handling Rabbits." Master Seminar 1 (2010). DVD: See page 94.

Photographs: upper, Bob Harriman; lower, Joy Gioia;

Grooming and Hygiene: *Ongoing health habits*

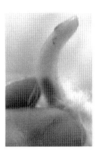

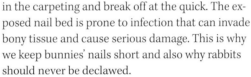

Separating toes for nail trimming, Anne Martin (far left) stands bunny on a padded table, while Christiana Merrit (below) sits bunny on her lap. Both are comfortable positions. Cut-off line is observable in white toenails (left). Use a flashlight to expose the vein in dark toenails. Face cleaning: (bottom) Susan Stark-Smith checks a towel-wrapped bunny.

PHYSICALLY-FIT RABBITS do a good job of self grooming but need help removing excess loose hair and cleaning difficult-to-reach areas. Most rabbits can't keep their toenails worn down and need to have them clipped regularly.

EAR CLEANING

Some rabbits also need help removing earwax. Otic chlorhexidine solution dissolves waxy buildup, which can then be swabbed out with cotton. Be careful not to push wax further into the ear canal. If you can't get all the wax out, you can soften it with your otic solution and let bunny shake the wax out herself. A dark crusty material inside the ears is usually a sign of ear-mites (see page 75).

FACE CLEANING

Eye infection, allergy, or even tooth-root problems may result in weepy eyes and wet cheeks (see page 78). Your vet will prescribe treatment for the eyes or teeth. To clean caked on debris from around the eyes, nose, or mouth, use cotton swabs and warm water. Wait for it to soak and soften, before gently combing it out.

TOENAIL CLIPPING

When bunny's toenails grow too long, they can catch in the carpeting and break off at the quick. The exposed nail bed is prone to infection that can invade bony tissue and cause serious damage. This is why we keep bunnies' nails short and also why rabbits should never be declawed.

Clip only the colorless part of the nail, avoiding the vein. Keep some styptic powder on hand to stop bleeding if the vein is accidentally nicked.

CARE OF THE COAT

Brushing or combing your rabbit keeps the coat clean and free of burrs, mats and stickers. Most caregivers have their favorite combs and brushes to remove loose hair and debris. To avoid scratching bunny's delicate skin, go gently with any kind of comb or brush with pointed teeth.

Long haired rabbits require daily brushing. For an extremely matted coat, use a matt splitter, not scissors, which can easily nick with the skin. If you must use scissors, put a fine-tooth comb between the flesh and the scissor blades so that no skin can be caught and snipped.

For shorter coats, a slicker brush is most commonly used for rabbits. Once the loose hair is removed, cornstarch or a cornstarch-based baby powder is nice dry shampoo for a bunny's coat.

Flea combing is essential for elderly or disabled

Brushing shelter bunnies at the Rabbit Center (above) is part of the upkeep shown by Cassandra Parshall.
Targeted cleaning of a small area is done with the bidet method under a water faucet (lower left). Spray-on cleansers or soaked cotton can also be used for small areas.
Broad cleaning of the hindquarters (lower right) is done with a shower hose attached to a water faucet.

rabbits. The fine teeth (page 76) remove small particles, dandruff, and insect eggs. Fly eggs, hidden in the coat, can be deadly if they hatch.

Use a brush to get tangles out before using a flea comb. When brushing an immobile rabbit, you may notice a lot of dandruff. You may suspect mites (check with your veterinarian), but more often it is due to diminished muscle and weight loss. As skin tissue shrinks, it sloughs off in small flakes.

CLEANING THE HINDQUARTERS

Some healthy and fully mobile rabbits have occasional problems with pasty stuck stool, dirty scent glands, or embedded debris. Avoid giving a full-body bath, or even dunking the lower half in water. Here are some much safer methods.

Bidet method. Bathing should be done on as small an area as possible. Bidet cleaning (under a running faucet) keeps the feet dry but soaks the hindquarters and tail. A mild, pH-balanced baby soap can be used to gently wash the soiled area.

Shower method. Rather than taking the bunny to the water spout, the shower method brings the water to the bunny through a shower hose. A dish drainer, partially covered by a towel, provides comfortable repose for the bunny, while leaving your hands free for the bathing activity. Soap-and-water cleaning requires thorough rinsing and drying.

Drizzle method. Small areas can be moistened by squeezing warm water-soaked cotton over a soiled spot. Give it a few minutes to loosen the hard material, which may fall off on its own, or it can be combed out. The most important cleaning tool that I've added to my arsenal in recent years is a seven-inch tapered barber's comb. Dipped in warm water it dampens and works out the debris from underneath instead of mashing it into the fur. The short-toothed tapered end can get into small crevices as well.

Human body cleansers can be safely used for rabbits in areas that can't be licked by the bunny or his companions. Otherwise, stick to chlorhexidine solution or plain water. If scent glands need cleaning, use cotton sticks and mineral oil or any nontoxic oil-based solution.   ■

The Well Kept Rabbit

BY SANDI ACKERMAN

THE KEY TO GIVING your rabbit the best chance for a long life is to provide a happy environment and to spot problems early. Here are some life-extending procedures.

Daily Routines

Hug your rabbit and as you do, become familiar with his body. You don't have to pick him up to do this, you can hug him while he and you are on the floor together. As you hug, feel him all over. Caress along his jaw line—then feel his tummy. Caress his head—then feel the crook of his legs and arms. Play "smushy face" with his entire head—then feel under his chin. You get the idea. Something that feels good—then something that may feel strange to him, at least the first few times you do this. He'll soon just think this is part of human behavior and will at first just put up with it but will soon learn to like this routine. What you are doing is getting used to the normal feel of his body, where his usual lumps and bumps are and how they feel on your healthy rabbit. Then, you'll be aware of any changes that might indicate a problem.

Check his litterbox looking for changes in the size or shape of his hard round droppings, which can indicate an intestinal problem. Seeing some hair strung between droppings is normal when he's shedding, but if you see very thick hair between the droppings then you should read about hairballs again, just to make sure you're doing all that you can to help him pass the hair out of his stomach. And of course, make sure that he's been urinating. If you find very thick white or grey urine for more than a day or two, he may have too much calcium in his diet, or hydration may be an issue.

Bonding and grooming go together. In order to keep hair from flying around your home and from being ingested by your rabbit, for just a couple of minutes every day comb or brush your rabbit. These short periods keep the experience pleasant for both of you. Within a short time he will likely began to look forward to these few minutes of daily bonding.

Other daily tasks include supplying fresh water and pellets, fresh veggies and small amounts of fruit, and plenty of hay.

Weekly Tasks

Clean his living area thoroughly.
Check eyes & nose to see that there is no discharge.
Check inside ears to see if they look clean far down inside.
Check bottom for cleanliness.

Every other Month

Clip nails.
Check bottom of feet for sores.
Check teeth to see that they're properly aligned.
Clean genital scent glands (one on either side of the genitals).
Check scent gland under the chin. As rabbits age this area can become infected.
Check for fleas.
Check for dandruff (could be indicative of fur mites).

Keeping up with these health-promoting tasks will mean a well kept rabbit. None of these things will take a lot of your time, but his time with you and the quality of both of your lives can be greatly increased. ■

A friendly chin rub gives you a chance to inspect the scent gland for lumps that might indicate infection..

Sandi Ackerman is Founder of Washington State's Best Little Rabbit Rodent and Ferret House in Seattle and Rabbit Meadows Sanctuary in Redmond.

Assisted Living: *Quality care for disabled bunnies*

Platform living on a table top suits Rudy (above) who gets comfortable on his pillow in the window sill. A padded desktop by a window (below) gives Dexter an enjoyable view. A floor pen works for Dylan (lower right), who can navigate with one stiff leg and get into a litterbox.

WHEN RABBITS LOSE MOBILITY, upright posture, or ability to reach and groom their extremities, they will need assistance with hygiene and their other daily tasks. Animals seem to have much less difficulty adjusting to loss of mobility than their humans do. Rabbits with crippling disease may stabilize and live comfortably for a prolonged period of time.

Millions of humans are on lifelong medication, for everything from allergies to heart disease, without question as to quality of life. We don't destroy humans who are missing a limb or have a physical impairment. So this is not the solution for an animal who is not in pain. My online article addresses several of these issues.[3]

HABITATS FOR DISABILITIES

Prepare a habitat for your impaired bunny that emphasizes safety, comfort, entertainment, and interaction. Pad the environment with fake fleece or pet bedding to prevent pressure sores, with wicking towels underneath and pillows of rolled rugs or towels along the perimeter.

Elevated solutions. Elevated living spaces provide convenience for the caregiver. By elevated I mean any housing arrangement that brings bunny up to your waist level. This could be a padded desktop, table, or any raised platform, preferably close to a window. Immobile rabbits appear to be entertained by watching birds and squirrels and even people doing yard work.

A low fence is sufficient for bunnies who can't hop. You want it high enough to be safe and low enough that you have easy access.

Floor setup. Bunnies with limited mobility can also use a comfortably furnished pen on the floor. Provide plenty of rolled-rug pillows to lean against. A floor habitat or pen is an amicable arrangement for bonded rabbits who have differing abilities.

3. Marinell Harriman, "Quality of Life," *House Rabbit Journal* II, no. 8 (1992), http://rabbit.org/quality-of-life/

Photograph: right, Rich Sievers

Leave the door open so that the able-bodied friends can go in and out.

Cage setup. Many immobile rabbits are perfectly happy in a cage with companions, Fosterer Donna Jensen keeps hers in groups, three–four to a cage in a triple-decker condo. "Although space is limited," she says, "they don't seem to mind, and they naturally bunch themselves together."

Furnishings. Special-needs setups include washable rugs, padded supports, flat dishes, water bottle, toys, companion(s), litterbox (maybe), and a nice view. If your disabled bunny spends supervised time outside, drape netting/screening over the pen to keep out against flies and mosquitoes.

FEEDING

Eating difficulties for some disabled rabbits are overcome by placing food within easy reach. They can eat the same hay, veggies, and pellets that are good for ambulatory rabbits. Frail, anorexic bunnies may need supplemental hand feedings of special formulas (page 60) prescribed by your vet.

Set out less perishable produce and hay for while you are away, and then give supplemental feedings when you are home. Set him next to his water bottle two–three times a day.

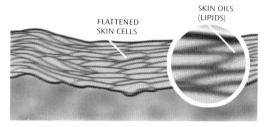

Figure 10.1: *Healthy Epidermal Barrier*
Skin pH is kept at 4.5–6.2

SKIN OILS (LIPIDS)
FLATTENED SKIN CELLS

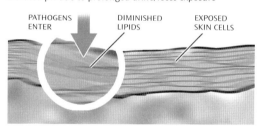

Figure 10.2: *Damaged Epidermal Barrier*
Elevated pH due to prolonged urine/feces exposure

PATHOGENS ENTER
DIMINISHED LIPIDS
EXPOSED SKIN CELLS

SKIN CARE

Urine scald is one of the most common problems encountered in rabbits who are unable to "posture" and thus project urine away from their bodies. Constantly soaked fur on any part of the body can result in painfully inflamed skin underneath. Shaving all at-risk areas allows you to monitor and treat the skin.

Preventing/treating scald begins in choosing a bathing technique that establishes a healthy epidermal barrier (shown above) that prevents pathogens from entering the body. To do this, the skin must be kept slightly acidic.

When bathing bunny's hindquarters (see page 84), always use a pH-balanced soap or cleanser.

Healthy skin (Figure 10.1): The outer layer of skin called the epidermal barrier consists of flattened skin cells (corneocytes) and skin oils (lipids). This layer is covered by a thin, slightly acidic, protective film known as the acid mantle (pH: 4.5– 6.2).

Damaged skin barrier (Figure 10.2): Acid mantle is disrupted by repeated cleanings, that raise pH. Skin pH is further raised by exposure to alkaline urine or fecal matter, which activate enzymes that damage the skin barrier and allow pathogens to penetrate skin cells.

Cozy cage living (upper left) is a good solution for disabled rabbits who thrive on intimacy and support each other in Donna Jensen's house.

Photograph: Donna Jensen; Skin diagrams: Bob Harriman

Cut to fit: (above) Punch a tail hole (optional) squarely in the middle of the diaper. Notch deeply into the leg edges at the front, making it curve around the legs.
Paws on counter (lower left) Bunny dangles while diaper is being fastened.
Hips on counter (lower right) Bunny reclines on back for diaper fastening.

After thorough drying, apply a moisture barrier/skin sealant to preserve lipids and keep urine or feces from penetrating skin cells. Moisture-barrier ointments used for bunnies are petrolatum or lanolin (no zinc). An all-in-one option is to douse the soiled area with a no-rinse, pH-balanced cleanser that contains lanolin. Human cleansers are safe on areas not licked by bunnies. Blot the cleansed area with soft tissue.

As damaged skin is repaired, a certain amount of sloughing is normal. The top layer of dead skin cells will slough off as new cells are building from underneath. The gentlest way to remove a sloughing layer is to massage it gently with the protective ointment to remove only the loose dead material.

WHEN TO USE DIAPERS

The main reason to diaper a bunny is to wick away moisture from tender flesh. Changing them three times a day is usually adequate. Use newborn size diapers. If your veterinarian recommends expressing your rabbit's bladder, you will be given a demonstration. There are varying techniques.

Diapers can be used frontwards or backwards, depending on where you want them fastened. The two front-wrapping methods that I use are illus-

trated in the photos. Other caregivers do equally well fastening the diaper at the back. Successful fitting, which keeps the diaper on, is done by notching the leg edges at the front. If you are turning the diaper backwards, make your notches at the back (which is now the front).

Do the appropriate cleaning each time you change the diaper. But first check for those vitamin-packed cecotropes and give them to bunny.

ACTIVITIES

If your bunny has lost any of his senses, provide activity for the others. If he can't see, turn on soft music. Provide toys that fit with bunny's abilities: some to toss, some to cuddle, some to chew, and some with wheels for mobility. Offer a variety of veggie treats and repeat the favorites. A compromised lifestyle doesn't have to mean misery.

Interaction with companions is the best therapy for an infirmed rabbit. Disabled rabbits are wonderful at taking care of each other. Most of the time, they accept partners readily. When I put them together, I use the simultaneous-petting technique (page 49). Donna Jensen adds Rescue Remedy (flower essence spray) for its calming effect.

There are many great tips available for improving the quality of care for special-needs bunnies. Amy Spintman brought many of these tips to us in her seminar presentation at the Rabbit Center.[4] Amy's website provides ongoing resources for caregivers,[5] as well as a link to a support group for disabled-rabbit care.[6] ∎

4. Amy Spintman, "Caring for Disabled Rabbits." Master Seminar 1 (2010). DVD: See page 94
5. http://www.catsandrabbitsandmore.com/disabled_rabbits
6. http://pets.groups.yahoo.com/group/disabledrabbits/

Newborn Care: *The first few weeks*

IF YOU COME ACROSS NESTING rabbits while hiking or doing yard work, don't assume they are orphans who need to be rescued. Read some advice from wildlife rehabbers, before you attempt to rescue them.[7] Help is more likely to be needed inside your home if an "accidental" litter is born.

A guaranteed way to prevent an accidental litter is to adopt already spayed/neutered rabbits from your shelter. The only way you will have an unintended litter is by having intact rabbits. If this event has already occurred, separate the father immediately (as females can get pregnant the day they give birth!) and give mama bunny some help with her nest. You will need to assemble:

A *nestbox* (about 12 x 14 inches). Cardboard will do temporarily, but it will get soggy and have to be replaced. The bottom should have a couple of drain holes. The sides can be about eight inches high, but the front should be no higher than four inches where mama bunny enters and exits.

Bedding. Line the box with a three-inch layer of clean yellow straw or finely shredded paper.

A fur-lined "well." Make a well in the middle of the nestbox and fill it with fur from the mother. If she hasn't pulled out fur herself, clip some.

The brood. Group the babies into this "well of fur" (yes, you can handle them). They will burrow to the bottom and stay there until mama bunny stands over them to nurse them.

Mama bunny. Show her where her babies are but don't expect her to get in there with them. Rabbits nurse once a day—usually very late at night or pre-dawn. Rabbit milk is very rich and can sustain the babies for 24 hours. If you weigh the babies daily on a postal or kitchen scale and they

Hand-raised orphans from the Hayward Animal Shelter await adoption.

are gaining weight, you can be sure that mama bunny is feeding them. See additional tips online.[8]

THE ORPHANED LITTER

The basic setup is similar for all baby bunnies. Additional care is needed for orphans, however, and provisions differ in several ways:

Bedding material that lines the nest box should consist of very clean cotton baby blankets or soft tee shirts, instead of straw or paper.

Sanitation is critical for orphans, who don't have antibody protection from their mother's milk. Wash your hands thoroughly before handling the babies, and sterilize feeding utensils.

Face and bottom cleaning with warm sterile water and cotton washes away spilled formula and stimulates elimination. Do this after every feeding.

7. Julie Smith, Susan Brown, and M. Wilson, "Orphaned Baby Bunnies: Wild and Domestic." HRS website, http://rabbit.org/faq-orphaned-baby-bunnies/

8. Sandy Koi, "Domestic Baby Bunnies and their Mom." HRS website, http://rabbit.org/domestic-baby-bunnies-and-their-mom/

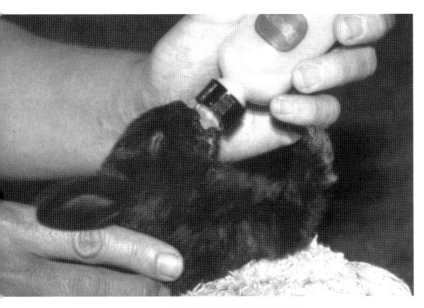

Bottle feeding can be successful only when the baby has retained a strong sucking reflex.

HAND FEEDING METHODS

You can bottle feed or syringe feed. Bottle feeding requires a perfect nipple. Carefully shave off some rubber at the end of the nipple. It's easier to punch the right size whole hole through thinner rubber. The hole should allow only a very fine spray. The babies' natural sucking motion closes the larynx and reduces the danger of aspiration.

With syringes the babies lap up the formula from the end of the syringe rather than draw with suction from a rubber nipple. Once started on syringes, they don't switch well to a bottle, because they lose their nursing reflex very quickly (within two days). Many wildlife rehabilitators prefer syringes, however, and feed only a few drops at a time to keep the liquid from entering the air passage. It does make sense to feed smaller amounts more often, since the formula is not as rich in fat and protein as mother's milk, and the babies become hungry more frequently.

WHAT TO FEED

Although I've used plain KMR (Kitten Milk Replacer) in the past, a more desirable formula, i.e., closer to the makeup of rabbit milk, can be found in Dana Krempel's comprehensive web article along with other valuable tips.[9]

Orphan-bunny formula

Fresh, whole goat milk (grocery store) ½ cup
Canned KMR (pet-food store) ½ cup
Freeze-dried colostrum (health food store) 1 tbsp
Heavy cream (grocery store) ½ tsp

Dana suggests mixing the batch a few hours in advance to allow the colostrum to soften. Colostrum is the ingredient in mother's milk that provides the babies with antibodies. These are approximate daily totals. Use less for smaller babies.

Table 9-1. *Orphan bunny intake*

AGE	AMOUNT	FREQUENCY	DAILY TOTAL
Newborn-1 week:	2.5 cc	2 x day	5 cc
1-2 weeks:	5-7 cc	2 x day	10–14 cc
2-4 weeks:	7-13 cc	2 x day	15-26 cc
4-7 weeks:	13-15 cc	2 x day	30 cc

Formula intake levels off around the 4th week, but continue to offer it in a dish, as the colostrum is still needed. Orphans can follow the basic "beginner" diet on page 59. However, small amounts of baby food (squash, pumpkin, applesauce), offered in a dish at about three weeks, might provide a safer transition to non-sterile whole foods (at about four weeks). They should be eating dry alfalfa hay a few days before starting clean wet greens. ■

9. Dana Krempels, "Care and Feeding of Orphaned Domestic Rabbits," http://www.bio.miami.edu/hare/orphan.html.

Caregiving: *The practical side*

After a few years of managing the living environment for ourselves and our rabbits, we learn ways to spend more time with our bunnies and less time on housework. There are many good reasons to organize our household tasks, so that they don't take over our lives.

TOOLS AND EQUIPMENT AIDS

By the time you add bunnies to your household, you have already acquired general cleanup equipment—brooms, mops, scrub brushes, and a vacuum cleaner. You also need to keep some convenient dedicated tools for the bunny area. These are my standard tools:

Containers for storing pellets, hay, and litter. I use large stackable plastic bins with side doors.

Litter scooper, squarish or rounded, depending on the contours of the litterbox.

Bottle brush with large and small brush-ends, for cleaning the water bottle, as well as the cap.

Whisk broom both long and short-handled with dustpans for small areas of bunny space.

Hand vacuum is obviously a versatile tool for fly-around hair and lightweight debris.

Paint scraper for residue on habitat floors.

Atomizers for white-vinegar spray. Use for cleaning the habitat area, as well as litterboxes.

Sponges, rags, or paper towels for wet jobs.

White vinegar (lots) is the all-purpose cleaner for rabbit areas. It is non-toxic to rabbits while it discourages the growth of bacteria. The acidity of the vinegar neutralizes the highly alkaline rabbit urine and prevents mineral buildup in litterboxes, and you can use it on carpeting, upholstery, or bedspreads.

Even with the best tools, you may need a break now and then. Caregivers are often advised, "Take care of yourself." This ensures that you will be there for your bunnies for many years. This advice includes getting away for a vacation or a weekend trip. Going away, however, is not restful if you are preoccupied with worry about your animals at home.

PET SITTERS TO THE (HUMAN) RESCUE

To put your mind at ease, line up a good pet sitter. If you don't have a friend who already knows your rabbit or who knows rabbits generally, ask for referrals from your veterinarian or your local HRS chapter. Some pet sitters do actual house-sitting. Others will come in at specified times to feed and exercise your animals. Competent pet-sitters are familiar with health issues of the species that they work with. Most can give injections and follow the plan prescribed by your veterinarian.

Cleaning items for large area (above left) can be pushed around on a cart.
***Supply corner:** (upper) large stacked bins store hay and litter. A long-handled whiskbroom and dustpan are used for spilled hay.*

Boarding pen at the Rabbit Center (above) allows ample space for exercise.
Camper option (right) is a fairly easy solution for traveling with special-needs bunnies
On the Road: Disabled bunnies Peanut, Molly, and Junior rest in their travel bed (inset).

BOARD WITHOUT BOREDOM

Often pet sitters can board your animal on their own premises with outstanding home care. Many humane societies and veterinary hospitals also offer boarding and have ample exercise space available. Before you sign up, ask to see the exercise facilities. Provide a printout of your bunnies' health histories and diet requirements, as well as a letter to your veterinarian or emergency clinic that authorizes your pet sitter to obtain any medical care necessary in your absence. With as many needs as possible anticipated in advance, you will have a much more relaxing time while away.

TRAVELING WITH BUNNIES

Most of us avoid taking our bunnies on airplanes unless absolutely necessary, such as a long-term relocation. Risks are too high for bunny to ride in cargo. Airlines constantly change their policies on allowing rabbits in the cabin, so it's always prudent to check with the airline in advance.

I had ruled out recreational land travel with bunnies for myself until watching Tracy Martin's presentation at the Rabbit Center.[10] Some rabbits are quite relaxed travelers and seem to enjoy the experience. They don't mind the noise and rattle of car travel on bumpy roads.

Tracy depicts tent camping, modes of transporting bunnies in baby trams on walking tours, and a set of guidelines for good etiquette while staying in hotels (which is important to help keep the hotels pet friendly).

Taking bunny with you is definitely a good option when you have immobile rabbits who need hand feedings, medications or a diaper change every few hours. Campers with built-in conven-

iences make special-needs care and comfort easy to manage. Margo DeMello and Tom Young take their three disabled rabbits and two dogs on camping trips regularly. They set up a fenced area a few steps outside their camper, where they can sit with their animals. This gives disabled bunnies, who can't go outside on their own, a chance to enjoy a change of scenery. ■

10. Tracy Martin, "Traveling with Rabbits." Master Seminar 2 (2010). DVD: See page 94.

Photographs: upper right and inset, Margo DeMello

Rabbit People: *How we define ourselves*

To be a true rabbit person, you must be more concerned that your bunnies are happy in their environment than you are with how well they meet your demands. You must have compassion, not only for your own bunnies, but for their kindred as well. You must want the best for all of them.

We rabbit people consider ourselves enlightened people, who are able to appreciate the intrinsic value of these often disregarded creatures. We care about what kind of lives they live, how appropriately their needs are met, and how humanely they are treated.

Rabbit people help each other because we care about other people's bunnies. We conscientiously share experiences and learn from each other. Rabbit people are anxious to get the best veterinary treatment available. Accumulating information on rabbits and seizing opportunities to educate the public, we are committed to elevating rabbits' status in the world.

More advanced rabbit people learn how to share their own space in a way that allows human and non-humans to live as equitably as possible. In her lecture at the Rabbit Center[11] and her article in the *House Rabbit Journal*,[12] Margo DeMello exposes us to a philosophy that exonerates us for being what unenlightened people consider foolish. We may not choose to live in a "normal" house but one that meets our bunnies' needs.

"Changing one's house to accommodate rabbits involves, at one level, trying to understand how rabbits see the world and a willingness to take up their culture as part of our own." Applying this philosophy involves compromises, "in the form of baby gates, wrappings for electrical wires, and a tolerance for ruined things."

As rabbit people, we take pride in our tolerance, as well as our bunnies' inventiveness in renovating their surroundings. We laugh with each other about their accomplishments. When we are praised for our patience, kindness, or compassion, we turn our attention to the animals who evoke these traits in us. In trying to define rabbit people, we find it's not about people at all. It's about the rabbits who take over our hearts and inspire us. ∎

In a perfect world created *by Margo DeMello, animals and humans converse on equal terms.*

11. Margo DeMello, "Living in a Rabbit's World." Master Seminar 2 (2010). DVD: See page 94.
12. Margo DeMello, "Human and Rabbit Coexistence," *House Rabbit Journal* V, no. 8 (2011)
   http://rabbit.org/rabbit-and-human-coexistence/

Photograph: courtesy Albuquerque Tribune

Notes

REFERENCES

Buddington, R. and J. Diamond. "Ontogenetic development of monosaccharide and amino acid transporters in rabbit intestine," *American Journal of Physiology* 259 (1990): 544-55.

Brown, Susan A. "Sluggish motility on the Gastrointestinal Tract." *House Rabbit Journal* III, no. 7 (1996). http://www.rabbit.org/journal/3-7/gi.html

Cheeke, P.R. *Rabbit Feeding and Nutrition.* Orlando: Academic Press, (1987).

Deeb, Barbara. Cardiovascular disease in rabbits. *House Rabbit Journal* IV, no.6 (2001)

Fraga, M. "Effect of type of fibre on the rate of passage and on the contribution of soft feces to nutrient intake of finishing rabbits." *Journal of Animal Science* 69 (1990):1566-74.

Gidenne, T. "Effect of fibre level, particle size and adaptation period on digestibility and rate of passage as measured at the ileum and in the faeces in the adult rabbit." *British Journal of Nutrition.* 67 (1992): 133-46

Lebas, F. (1980). "Les recherches sur l'alimentation du lapin: Evolution au cours de 20 dernieres annees et perspectives d'avenir." Adapted by P. Cheeke. *Rabbit Feeding and Nutrition.* Academic Press, (1987).

McLaughlin, C.A. and R.B. Chaisson. *Laboratory Anatomy of the Rabbit.* William C. Brown, (1990): 59-64

Percy, D.H. and S.W. Barthold. *Pathology of Laboratory Rodents and Rabbits.* Ames, Iowa: Iowa State University Press, (1993).

Sakaguchi, E. . "Digesta retention and fibre digestion in brushtail possums, ringtail possums and rabbits." *Comparative Biochemistry and Physiology* 96A (1990):351

RECOMMENDED READING

You can find any of the following books by running a general web search or by searching House Rabbit Society's website at http://rabbit.org.

Biology and Medicine of Rabbits and Rodents. by John E. Harkness, Patricia V. Turner, Susan VandeWoude, Colette L. Wheler

Ferrets, Rabbits Rodents by Katherine E. Quesenberry and James W. Carpenter

Stories Rabbits Tell by Susan E. Davis and Margo DeMello

Rabbits: Gentle Hearts, Valiant Spirits by Marie Mead with Nancy LaRoche

Textbook of Rabbit Medicine by Frances Harcourt-Brown

Rabbit Health in the 21st Century by Kathy Smith.

When Your Rabbit Needs Special Care by Lucile C. Moore and Kathy Smith

The Relaxed Rabbit: Massage for Your Pet Bunny by Chandra Moira Beal

Why Animals Matter: The Case for Animal Protection by Erin E. Williams and Margo DeMello

Why Does My Rabbit...? by Anne McBride

When Only the Love Remains by Emily Stuparyk

Dining at the Leaf and Twig Cafe: The Hay-Intensive Diet for Pet Rabbits, Guinea Pigs and Chinchillas by Judy Hardin.

FOR YOUR DVD LIBRARY

Nail-Trimming and Handling, by Mary Cotter; New York City Chapter of the House Rabbit Society, 2001, DVD. If you don't already have this video, you can order it from http://www.rabbitcare.org/video.htm.

The Rabbit Center's Hop Shop has a great collection of DVD recordings from the Master Seminars of 2010. To order any of the DVD sets, go to http://rabbit.org/rabbit-center/ and then click "Hop Shop Online."

Seminar 1: Enhanced Rabbit Health, presented by Dana Krempels, Joy Gioia, Judith Pierce, Amy Spintman; DVD, 3-disc set (6 hours). Topics include digestive problems, emergency, medicating, handling, disabilities, enrichment, and alternative medicine.

Seminar 2: Advanced Rabbit Speake, presented by Nancy LaRoche, Kit Jagoda, Tracy Martin, Karen Courtemanche, and Margo DeMello; DVD, 3-disc set (6 hours). Topics include seeing/hearing, emotions, predator proofing, bonding, multiple animals, and traveling.

Seminar 3: Rabbit Ingestibles, presented by Susan Smith, George Flentke, Dawn Sailer-Fleeger, and Kristen Strobel; DVD, 4-disc set (8 hours). Topics include nutrition, drugs, toxins, diagnostics, parasites, dental disease, and geriatrics.

ONGOING RESOURCE

Your first online contact for in-depth information should be http://rabbit.org. From there you can link to rabbit information and resources all over the world.

House Rabbit Society International headquarters: 148 Broadway, Richmond, CA 94804. 510.970.7575

Index

DATE DUE

920   Bentley, Karen.
BEN   The Unsers

THE UNSERS

THE UNSERS

Karen Bentley

with additional text by Jeff Gluck

CHELSEA HOUSE
PUBLISHERS

Cover Photo: Race car legend Al Unser Jr. drives the No. 31 Kelley Racing Toyota Dallara during practice for the 2003 Purex Dial Indy 200 at the Phoenix International Raceway in Phoenix, Arizona.

CHELSEA HOUSE PUBLISHERS

VP, New Product Development   Sally Cheney
Director of Production   Kim Shinners
Creative Manager   Takeshi Takahashi
Manufacturing Manager   Diann Grasse

STAFF FOR THE UNSERS

Editorial Assistant Sarah Sharpless
Production Editor Bonnie Cohen
Photo Editor Pat Holl
Series Design and Layout Hierophant Publishing Services/EON PreMedia

Original edition first published in 1996.
© 2006 by Chelsea House Publishers.

http://www.chelseahouse.com

First Printing

1   3   5   7   9   8   6   4   2

Library of Congress Cataloging-in-Publication Data

Bentley, Karen.
   The Unsers / Karen Bentley with additional text by Jeff Gluck.
      p. cm.—(Race car legends. Collector's edition)
   Includes bibliographical references and index.
   ISBN 0-7910-8764-6
   1. Unser family—Juvenile literature. 2. Automobile racing drivers—United States—
Biography—Juvenile literature. I. Gluck, Jeff, 1980- II. Title. III. Series.
GV1032.A1B415 2005
796.72'092'2–dc22

2005010506

TABLE OF CONTENTS

THE LEGEND CONTINUES: THE 1992 INDIANAPOLIS 500

The Indianapolis 500, the biggest event of race-car driving and one of the biggest sporting events in the world, was almost over. Only 11 laps of the 1992 race remained out of the 200 total laps in the 500-mile event. Half a million fans roared with excitement in the stands surrounding the Indianapolis Motor Speedway on that Memorial Day weekend, and millions more watched the race on television.

Michael Andretti, of the renowned Andretti racing family, shot his black-and-white Ford-powered race car into Lap 189 of the asphalt Indy track. He had led for 163 of the first 189 laps and was comfortably ahead by several car lengths of Al Unser Jr. in second place.

This race had already been the wildest Indy 500 in the race's 76-year history. Ten crashes had taken out 13 drivers, injuring three seriously. Only 12 drivers of the 33 cars that started managed to finish the race at all on that cold, overcast day in Indianapolis, Indiana.

Al Unser Jr. wanted terribly to beat Michael Andretti. One reason was the $1,244,184 first-place prize. Al Jr. had

Eddie Cheever, Michael Andretti, and Mario Andretti lead here at the start of the 1992 Indianapolis 500, but it was the Unser family that would make history on this day.

never won the Indianapolis 500, and enormous pressure was on him to win. Although he was only 30 years old, this was his tenth Indy 500 attempt. His uncle, Bobby, and his father, Al Unser Sr., had racked up seven Indy 500 victories between them: three for Uncle Bobby (in 1968, 1975, and 1981), and four for Al Sr. (in 1970, 1971, 1978, and 1987). The Unsers had become the most successful Indy 500 racing family ever. Winning at the Indy 500 had become a family tradition.

The only other family that repeatedly competed at Indianapolis was the Andretti family: Mario, his two sons Michael and Jeff, and nephew John. After a combined 43 starts at the Indianapolis Motor Speedway, only Mario had ever won the checkered flag, in 1969.

The Andretti streak of misfortune at the Indy 500 continued in 1992. On Lap 79, Mario Andretti hammered his car into the concrete outside wall, breaking toes on both feet. Jeff also smacked the outside wall, on Lap 110, and broke bones in his legs, ankles, and feet. Both men were hospitalized. Mario was back to racing in a matter of weeks. Jeff would require months of rehabilitation.

But Michael Andretti was running extremely well. Late in the race, he seemed to have the victory sewn up. Al Unser Jr. was trying out a new car, and it had performed so poorly in practice—the engine blew on the second day—that he didn't think he'd win. Still, with 12 laps to go in the race, he had just whipped around 30-year-old Canadian Scott Goodyear's blue-and-silver Lola-Chevy (Lola chassis, Chevy engine) to move into second place.

Al Unser Sr. drove his Lola-Buick up into fourth place. Although he set a record for the most laps led at the Indianapolis 500, Al Sr. had come to the 1992 Indy 500 without a decent ride. He only got a chance to race when a rookie was injured in practice. He was racing very well for someone who was driving an unfamiliar car. But he seemed to pose no threat to Andretti, who had mopped up the field for most of the race.

The Indy cars were averaging 220 miles per hour on the straightaways and 200 miles per hour on the corners. They were flying around the 2.5-mile oval track in about 45 seconds. Al Sr. and Bobby Unser had taught Al Jr. well. Al Sr. had a reputation as a patient driver who was very good in long

Al Unser Jr. is shown in 1987, the same year his father, Al Sr., won his fourth Indianapolis 500. Al Jr. continued the family tradition by winning his first Indy in 1992.

races like the Indy 500: he paced himself and saved the car, not running it harder than he had to. In contrast, Bobby Unser drove every lap like it was the last lap of the race, and Al Jr. drove hard when he needed to but also paced himself.

Suddenly, 11 laps from the finish line, Michael Andretti's car slowed. A fuel pump drive belt had broken. In a split second the race was over for him. The fabled "Andretti bad luck" had struck again.

"It can't get much worse than this," Michael Andretti said after he bailed out of his broken half-million-dollar car. "This place is cruel, so cruel."

Al Unser Jr. took the lead in his red, white, blue, and black Chevy after Andretti's car coasted to a stop at the side of the track.

"I felt for Mikey," he said. "But a second later, I had Scott Goodyear right up my tailpipe."

Goodyear (who is no relation to members of the tire company family) had started the race last but managed to move up to 20th place after just eight laps. He'd expertly worked his way up to third place, then took second after Andretti was out of the race. That kind of maneuvering through traffic was extremely difficult in this Indy 500. Goodyear and the other drivers had to dodge debris from the almost constant wrecks that littered the track.

The unseasonably cold weather caused most of the carnage. Many wrecks happened soon after pit stops, when the drivers pull the cars off the track to refuel and get new tires. After each pit stop the cars' new, cold racing slicks, or tires, had to be carefully "scuffed" through a series of tight, wiggly maneuvers so that they would properly grip the track. But to do that, the drivers had to move slowly out of pit stops and take the time to warm up the tires.

The cars were prepared wrong for the race-day weather, too. In the final practice the Thursday before the race, the laps had been run in sunny, 80-degree temperatures. The mechanics had adjusted their cars for a hot, sticky track. Then the temperature dropped into the 50s on Sunday, race day. The conditions were so bad that one driver, Roberto Guerrero, spun into the wall on the second parade lap, before the race had even officially begun. Guerrero had set a track record in

Skid marks and tire impact markings on the wall of the first turn give evidence of the number of crashes during the 1992 Indy 500.

practice of four laps averaging 232.482 miles per hour, but on race day his tires were inadequately warmed up.

Al Jr. started the race 12th. Like Goodyear, he nimbly picked his way through the traffic. He was 10th after 100 miles, fifth after 200, fourth after 300, and third after 400. "I was warming up my tires from the beginning of the race," Unser said. "I was extremely careful."

Goodyear and Al Jr. drove furiously for the finish. On the last few laps of the race Goodyear tried again and again to pass. Their cars seemed tied together by puppet strings. Al dove to the inside of the track around corners. Goodyear dove after him. Al zigged to the outside of the track on straightaways. Goodyear zagged after him.

Unser, the more experienced driver, was expertly using a lot of track to prevent Goodyear from getting behind him in his draft. If Goodyear had been able to get in Unser's tow, he might have been able to swing around Unser for the pass. "Experience is hard to get and hard to beat," remarked Owen Snyder, team manager at Galles International Racing, which supported Unser's 1992 Indy 500 run.

"I don't call what Al Jr. did blocking; I call it using a lot of racetrack," Goodyear diplomatically said later. Deliberately blocking another car is illegal in Indy-car racing.

On the final turn before the checkered flag flashed down to signal the end of the race, Unser's car slid dangerously. He backed off the throttle—the other choice was to spin into the concrete wall outside the track. Goodyear saw his chance and tried to slip around Unser on the inside.

Unser fought him off. "I tried to make the race car as wide as I could. I was talking to it, saying, 'Come on. Let's go!'" he said.

Racing at over 220 miles per hour on the final straightaway, Unser managed to block Goodyear until the last 100 yards of the race. Then, in a burst of speed, Goodyear swept around Unser's car on the inside.

"He got a run on me like you wouldn't believe. He gave me one heckuva scare that he was going to take it away then," Al Jr. said. "I moved over a little bit to block but finally decided to move straight on, and that the best man was going to win. Scott was right under my exhaust."

Al Jr. blazed across the finish line 0.043 of a second— about half a car length—ahead of Scott Goodyear to win the closest Indy 500 ever.

Al's average speed was slow for an Indy 500—134.479 miles per hour. The average speed had been reduced by

Al Unser Jr. (No. 3) leads Scott Goodyear (No. 15) in the 1992 Indianapolis 500. Al Jr. won by 0.043 of a second—the closest finish in the history of the race.

yellow caution flags, when the drivers must slow down while debris from accidents is cleared from the track.

"Very seldom does the fastest car win the race in the Indy 500. Al Jr.'s not always the fastest guy, but at the end of the race you look, and there he is. He never gives up—that's the thing that makes him special," said Owen Snyder.

"What my father has instilled in me is that only one lap is what you want to lead, and that's the last lap," Al Jr. said.

Al Sr. was the only other driver to complete the 200 laps of the 1992 Indy 500, placing third. With Al Jr.'s win, they became the first father–son winning combination at the Indy 500.

When his son took the checkered flag, the usually unemotional Al Sr. broke down. "To love something as much as I love racing," he said, "and then to have your son come along and win here is the greatest feeling there is."

"Indy means life to me. I've been trying to do this since I was a little boy. This is just a dream come true," Al Jr. said simply.

After the race he returned to his motor home, parked just outside the track. A sign had been painted in yellow on the windshield, proclaiming, "There is a God!"

The sign seemed to mean that Unser had been watched over in the race, unlike the hapless Andrettis. Or maybe it meant that he had joined the pantheon of race-car gods who have won at Indianapolis.

DID YOU KNOW?

The Unser family has won a total of nine Indianapolis 500 races. That means the Unsers are quite used to drinking the traditional jug of milk after winning the prestigious race.

Every year, the Indy 500 winner drinks milk in Victory Lane. The tradition started in 1936 when the race winner, Louis Meyer, drank some milk for refreshment after the race.

According to the Indy 500 Website, "An executive with what was then the Milk Foundation was so elated when he saw the moment captured in a photograph in the sports section of his newspaper the following morning that he vowed to make sure it would be repeated in coming years."

The rest is history.

②

"BOBBY DROVE HARD, ALL THE TIME"

The famous Unser racing family began their association with cars around the turn of the century. Then, Louis Unser, grandfather of Bobby and Al Sr., began to make his living as a mechanic in Colorado Springs, Colorado.

Louis's three sons—Louis Jr., Jerry, and Joe—made a name for themselves by riding two motorcycles and a side-car to the top of Colorado's Pike's Peak in the 1920s. This mountain is 14,110 feet high and stands out at the edge of the Great Plains as a sign that the Rocky Mountains are nearby. Pike's Peak has always been considered a challenge to hike up, and for many years no one thought to try to drive up it. For one thing, the road stopped three quarters of the way to the top.

In the first race up Pike's Peak about 40 drivers competed with the Unsers. All the others turned back. The Unsers won by default.

Soon after the Unsers drove up Pike's Peak through the rocks and brush, Spencer Penrose, a local philanthropist, built the rest of the road and began to sponsor a yearly race up the mountain. That race up Pike's Peak, sometimes called Unsers' Peak, became a proving ground for Unser drivers.

Lou Unser finishes a trial heat in the 1949 Pike's Peak Hill Climb. Wanting "to beat Uncle Louis" in the Pike's Peak Hill Climb motivated Bobby Unser to get into racing.

Jerry Unser, the father of Bobby and Al Sr., always built and worked on the cars he drove. He was also a pilot, doing barnstorming shows—flying across the country and performing stunts, mostly in rural areas. Then he lost his license for souping up the engines of his airplanes in violation of federal regulations. Eventually he became a movie stunt driver.

Jerry and his third wife, Mary, had four sons: twins Jerry Jr. and Louie, Bobby (15 months younger), and Al (five years younger than Bobby). Jerry moved his family from Colorado Springs to Albuquerque, New Mexico, in 1936 and opened a garage and filling station on Route 66. "Daddy could fix things nobody else could," Bobby remarked.

All four Unser boys quickly graduated from riding wild burros they caught on the mesa outside Albuquerque to driving Model A Fords. When Bobby Unser was just 8 years old, he was already driving his Model A on the dirt mesa roads near his home.

By the time Jerry and Louie were 16 years old and Bobby was 15, they had moved on to drive race cars. They established themselves as a force on the local short tracks across New Mexico, Colorado, and Arizona.

The Unsers were aggressive competitors in and out of race cars. "Several times we had to back out of a racetrack because we were fighting," Louie admitted. "A couple of times we had to leave before the police arrived."

Jerry Jr. was the first Unser to become a national champion: United States Auto Club (USAC) stock car champion in 1957. "He was the first really big thing to come out of Albuquerque," said Louie, who made a career on the West Coast building race-car engines. In 1958, Jerry was also the first Unser to make it to the Indy 500. But in 1959, Jerry crashed on the first day of practice there and was badly burned. "He had what they call third-degree burns," said Louie. "But really they don't have a number to describe how bad he was burned over his back and legs and kidneys."

Although race-car driving will always be an extremely dangerous sport, today's Indy cars are safer. The wheels are made to fall off so that cars now skid down the track instead of flipping over. Methanol is used as fuel instead of gasoline because methanol ignites less quickly, reducing the risk of fire. (The only problem with methanol fuel is that the dim blue flames of a methanol fire are hard to see—sometimes a driver can be invisibly on fire.) In a fire, the fire-resistant suits drivers wear give them about 30 seconds of protection.

Jerry died 17 days later of pneumonia and kidney failure. With today's modern medicine, he would have stood

Jerry Unser Jr., the first Unser driving champion, waves from his roadster at Pike's Peak, Colorado in 1957. Two years later, Jerry crashed during practice for the Indianapolis 500 and died, days later, from his injuries. Today, better safety features are built into race cars and drivers wear flame-retardant suits to reduce some of the danger.

a better chance. In 1959, kidney dialysis machines, which help a person survive kidney failure, were still primitive.

In those days, deaths at the track were common—some say half of all drivers died due to accidents. Jerry's death, although a personal tragedy for the Unsers, did not affect their racing style. He had taken the same risks they all did.

After Jerry's death, Bobby Unser, who along with his younger brother Al would make race-car history, emerged as the Unser to beat in racing. Bobby began his career racing stock cars in New Mexico at age 15. At 16, he won the Southwest Modified Stock Car Championship.

Some of Bobby's early victories were achieved under harrowing circumstances. At Speedway Park in Albuquerque in 1951, Bobby was running third in a stock-car race behind older, more experienced drivers. Then the frontrunner's car burst into a spectacular gasoline fire that lit up the entire track. Bobby took the lead and won.

When he was 17, still not old enough to hold a competition license, Bobby drove his father's car in the annual Pan-American Road Race, from Tuxtla Gutierrez at the south end of Mexico to Juarez in the north. His father started the race and then changed places with underage Bobby. "Daddy and I could change seats while still on the move," Bobby said.

Later that same year, 1951, Bobby was at Pike's Peak, determined to make a name for himself at the race. "My uncle Louis told me that if I came up to Pike's Peak for practice, he would let me drive his car on roads off the mountain," Bobby said. But his uncle ran the car himself every day. "I became kind of bitter," Bobby commented.

Discouraged and completely out of money, he and a friend left for home. The only way they could get there with no money was to siphon gas from vehicles they found along the way. Siphoning gas was an art: not every tank the two friends tried was full, and so they usually had to raid several tanks to fill up their own. "In those days it would have been nothing for some guy to poke a gun out the window of his house and shoot you," Bobby said.

Just as Bobby and his friend pulled into Pueblo, Colorado, they saw a race car being towed the other way. They followed the car to the track in Pueblo. Once there, Bobby put on his racing jacket and told the officials he was a racing champion from New Mexico. That was sufficient to get himself and his friend free pit passes. Once they could approach the crews, Bobby found a car to drive in the race, despite the fact that he was still only 17 and underage. However, he had a fake birth certificate stating that he was 22, a year older than the legal age to drive in the race.

Bobby won at Pueblo. The two jubilant friends headed for home. They now had the princely sum of $80, enough for food, a motel, and gas (in those days gas cost about 15 or 20 cents a gallon).

It was still a while longer before the Unsers became the wealthy, famous family that they are today. In 1955, Bobby lived in a tiny house in the desert at the edge of Albuquerque. "We used to raise centipedes and black widows in that house," Bobby remembered. "When the sand would blow really bad, sometimes we would just open the doors and let it blow on through."

Bobby Unser would return to Pike's Peak. In 1955, Bobby's first year racing there, he placed fifth. Louie and Jerry placed third and fourth respectively, Louie in a car Bobby loaned him. In the Pike's Peak race the next year, Bobby was driving the car he had loaned Louie the year before. The three Unser brothers were running against famous drivers Bob Finney and Slim Roberts, who were racing cars for Dick Frenzel's big-time operation out of Denver, Colorado. "I was definitely favored not to win," Bobby said.

That year, 1956, was when the Unsers began to change racing at Pike's Peak. The Jaguar engines in their cars were small compared to big-league V-8s run by Frenzel. But the Unsers' cars were lighter. Their Jaguar engines turned more

Bobby Unser, all-time winner of the Pike's Peak Hill Climb, is pictured standing next to the car he drove over the treacherous 12.5 miles of dirt roads that wind up the mountain. Pike's Peak can be seen in the background.

revolutions per minute (rpm), and Jerry Sr. had invented a special racing camshaft for them. Both improvements provided more power at higher speeds. The Unser cars' engines were also a bigger, more powerful 3.8-liter instead of the standard 3.5-liter engine.

Bobby Unser won the race. "That race was a storybook affair," he remarked. "That was the turnaround in my career. I became a famous person overnight."

He went on to win at Pike's Peak for six years in a row, from 1958 through 1963. In all but one race he set records. Finally, in 1986, he topped Uncle Louis's nine victories at the mountain. Bobby Unser now has a record 13 Pike's Peak titles.

"The Unser brothers raced at Pike's Peak to beat each other and most of all to beat Uncle Louis," Bobby said. "That was what got me into racing—not to win the Indianapolis 500 three times but to beat Uncle Louis."

Although he achieved his goal of beating Uncle Louis, Bobby Unser also won the Indy 500 three times: in 1968, 1975, and 1981. "To win at Indy is a function of not making any mistakes all day long," Bobby remarked. "You need a good game plan and good thinking—you have to be at a peak in your performance."

His first Indy 500 win, in 1968, was in record time against hard competition. Three turbine cars—cars with jet engines—were in the race. The turbine feature seemed to give these drivers a big advantage over the rest of the field.

One turbine-car driver was killed in practice before the race. Bobby Unser then battled the remaining two. His brother, Al Sr., was also in the race. About halfway to the finish, Al's car lost a wheel and hit the wall. Al climbed to the top of the wall and waved to Bobby, signaling that he was okay.

Bobby had managed to lead over half of that Indy 500, but then he broke a gearshift lever. From then on he had only one gear—fourth. (After a stop a car usually moves through first, second, and third gears to work up speed.) "It took a long time to get that sucker going after pit stops," Bobby remarked. The broken lever caused him to lose almost a full lap every time he pitted.

With 32.5 miles to go in the 1968 Indianapolis 500, Joe Leonard's turbine car rolls to a halt. Bobby Unser whips past to win the checkered flag.

But the turbine cars were also having problems. The team's sponsor, an oil company, was running them on gasoline instead of jet fuel. The gasoline was an oil-company product, and having the race cars run on it was good publicity.

"The drivers had to back out the power of their engines to bring down the temperature of the gasoline fuel," Bobby said. "Now they were playing in my playground."

At the dash to the finish after the last pit stop, Joe Leonard was leading in his turbine. Art Pollard, driving another turbine, blocked Unser, keeping him back in second.

Suddenly, with only about 15 laps to go, first Leonard's, then Pollard's car slowed to a stop. The cars' engine-fuel pumps had seized up. The reason was that gasoline is a poor lubricant, unlike jet fuel.

Unser had no other competition in the race. The 400,000 people in the stands rose to their feet, cheering. He coasted to his first Indianapolis victory.

Success didn't come without a price, though. In a 1973 Indy-car race at Phoenix, Unser suffered his worst and most spectacular wreck ever. "I was leading the race," he said, "and passing Gary Bettenhausen, who was a lap down. He pushed me into the wall. That first hit wasn't so bad. But my car spun and hit another wall. The car disintegrated."

In the past 20 years the safety features added to Indy cars make such a complete wipeout less likely. An Indy car must weigh at least 1,550 pounds, whereas the Formula One cars, a fast European kind of race car, weigh only 1,150 pounds. Most of the extra Indy-car weight is added as safety features, such as increased reinforcement around the driver.

"That was such a bad-looking wreck, even the firemen wouldn't come near it—they were afraid it was going to explode," Bobby continued. "But I needed help. I couldn't get out of the car because I was broken up all over. My shoulder was broken, both feet, every one of my ribs on both sides."

Bobby's brother Al was in the same race. The brothers often raced against each other in the same races, on different teams, and it was their policy not to stop when the other crashed. But this time Al stopped. "The first guy who got to me was my brother," Bobby said. Al pulled Bobby out of the car, taking himself out of the race.

"Al went in the helicopter with me," Bobby said. "But at the hospital no doctors were waiting. They put me in a holding room. I was hurting so bad, it was unbelievable. I'd wake up, then go unconscious again. Finally Al grabbed a doctor walking down the hall by the shirt and just dragged him into the room."

Bobby was taken to the X-ray room. The technicians moved the machine above Bobby's eyes to begin total-body X-rays. Suddenly one of the machine's rubber cables caught fire, and hot rubber dripped toward his face. The technicians took off running. But because of his severe injuries, Bobby couldn't move.

Al was leaning up against the wall outside the room. When he saw the technicians run out, he hurried inside, pushed the machine away from Bobby's face, and wheeled his brother back into the hallway.

"For a couple of days they didn't know if I was going to make it or not," Bobby said. "My neck was swollen so badly, it was pinching off the blood running up and down the jugular vein." He never did get X-rays. "I didn't know my feet were broken until I tried to walk on them." His broken bones finally mended, although crookedly, without treatment.

Serious wrecks are common for a race-car driver, especially one with Bobby Unser's racing style. He developed a reputation as an uncompromisingly aggressive driver.

"He drove hard, all the time," said Owen Snyder of Galles International Racing.

"That pretty much describes my central philosophy," Bobby agreed.

Unser always pushed himself and his team almost to the breaking point. "Total commitment is what a race-car driver needs more than good eyesight or raw talent," he said. "And concentration: Not many drivers can concentrate all the way through a race, although they think they can."

Bobby Unser also worked on his cars. Sometimes these experiments resulted in mechanical or tactical failure. But it is likely that he won more races by always searching for more speed or a greater technical advantage.

The tactic paid off in the 1968 Indy 500. Bobby had bought and introduced a new turbocharged engine for his first Indy win instead of going with a safer, older Ford engine.

In 1982, at the age of 48, Bobby Unser retired from driving Indy cars. He has been married four times and has

Did you know?

Indy cars are unique vehicles that can travel over 220 mph. But with such complex machines, there are many traits that can't be found on a normal car.

For example, an IRL car can go from 0 to 100 mph in under three seconds, while the fastest regular car takes 12 seconds to get to that speed. That's partly because Indy cars can produce four times the horsepower of a regular car.

If you were driving an Indy Racing League (IRL) car on the highway, you would have to stop at the gas station all the time. The reason is that Indy cars use 1.3 gallons of gas per lap when they race at Indianapolis Motor Speedway.

When Indy cars are at full speed, it takes less than one second to drive the length of an entire football field. Considering that remarkable statistic, it's not surprising to learn that the tires on an Indy car rotate 43 times per second.

four children: Bobby Jr., Cindy, Robby, and Jeri. He also worked as a sportscaster for ABC Sports Television.

His retirement from Indy cars was by no means the end of his driving career. In 1993 he set a new land-speed record of 223.709 miles per hour in a D gas-modified roadster, a class of cars run in the famous international road race at Bonneville Salt Flats in Utah. That same year he won the Fastmasters invitational race for drivers over 50, driving identical Jaguar XJ 220s, and took home $115,000. In 1994, he was inducted into the International Motorsports Hall of Fame.

His Fastmasters victory was never much in doubt: Unser led the entire 12-lap race. He had the second-fastest average time in practice laps and began the race in the front row, on the outside. That was a good position, but not as good as the inside front-row position George Folmer had qualified for on the narrow track.

"Somebody will have to give on that first turn," Bobby commented.

"I guarantee you, Bobby ain't givin' up nothin'," the sportscaster predicted correctly.

AL SR.: "HE WAS FAST RIGHT OFF THE BAT"

"**F**or me to want or even think about being better than my father would be presumptuous. If I could stay one step behind my father throughout my entire life, then I would be a successful person," Al Jr. remarked. "I've said this as a kid, and I still mean it today: My dad is one of the greatest racing drivers who ever lived, and his record shows it."

Al Unser Sr. won the Indianapolis 500 four times: in 1970, 1971, 1978, and 1987. With four wins, he is tied with Rick Mears and A.J. Foyt for the most wins in the Indy 500. He is also one of five drivers to win two consecutive Indy 500s (the others were Wilbur Shaw, 1939–40; Mauri Rose, 1947–48; Bill Vukovich, 1953–54; and Helio Castroneves, 2001–02).

Al Sr. started racing at age 17. "He was fast right off the bat," said his older brother Bobby. Al won the first race he ever entered, at Speedway Park in Albuquerque, in a stock car built by his father and Bobby. Soon he had a string of victories.

Other drivers started picking on him. "Grownups don't like kids to outrun them," Bobby remarked. "So I started racing with Al. He and I would take turns who was going to

Al Unser Sr. celebrates his fourth Indianapolis 500 win in 1987. At nearly 40 years old, he was the oldest driver to ever win the race at that time.

win each race. We could dictate, because we were far faster than anyone else. If anyone gave us trouble after the race, we'd fight them. We put out a message: Don't screw with the Unsers.

"Al and I have always gone down the same roads," Bobby added. "Not lying, not stealing, not cheating—we got the same things from our parents." Nevertheless, the two Unser brothers have very different personalities: Bobby's way with words once resulted in a job as an ABC sportscaster, whereas Al Sr.'s reluctance to speak is legendary.

Al won his first Pike's Peak race in 1964, setting a new course record and breaking Bobby's six-race winning streak. The Pike's Peak races were the real contest between Al and Bobby. "He'd build his car over on one side of the street and I'd build mine on the other," said Bobby. "I couldn't go over to see his, and he couldn't come over to see mine. So we'd go to the racetrack and see who had done his best thinking and best homework.

"It would get tense between me and Al about who would win, but it never stayed. We were able to separate business and family—we never really got in a fight. We never let it come down to anything other than racing. Even though he's my brother, we can't be brothers on the racetrack. It took a lot of work and practice to keep it that way. We never talked about racing—not about secret things. He would never try to pump me for secrets and I would never try to pump him."

The next step for an Unser after a Pike's Peak win was to make a run at Indianapolis. "When I was a kid, every year when the Indianapolis was run, I was glued to the radio, and I said that someday I would be there," Al said. His first run at the Indy 500, in 1965, was in a car owned by A.J. Foyt. Al placed ninth, not bad considering he had started in the last row.

The more Al learned about Indy, the better he did. In 1966, he was running third when he wrecked his car. The following year, he came in second, behind Foyt.

Bobby won the 1968 race. "I was happy for him, but jealous of him. You want your brother to do good, but I guess you're not human if you don't want to do better. We both wanted to be the first Unser to win Indy and he got there first."

Al's car was hot in 1969, and he was the favorite to win. But the day before qualifying began, Al broke his leg while driving a motorcycle in the parking lot. "Missing Indianapolis that year was the biggest disappointment in my life. I'd not only let myself down, but everyone who'd worked on the car."

He didn't have long to wait to get back to winning. Al won five races that year after the cast came off. And in 1970, he claimed the pole position at Indianapolis. Johnny Rutherford and A.J. Foyt were right beside him at the start of the race, but Unser quickly pulled away.

At mile 120, Lloyd Ruby took the lead. Ten laps later, oil spurted into his exhaust pipe; his car became a flaming torch, and he had to retire. Unser regained the lead and never relinquished it. After 200 miles, he came up on A.J. Foyt, who was in second place. Instead of passing, Unser slipped his blue-and-gold P.J. Colt-Ford behind Foyt's car; for the next 200 miles Foyt raced all out and Unser drafted behind him. Foyt suffered a broken gear box in avoiding a crash and finished tenth. Unser and his Johnny Lightning "500" Special cruised on to win by 32 seconds over his nearest competitor. He became the first pole sitter to win the race since 1963.

The 1970 race was the first to feature a total purse of over one million dollars. Unser also set a record with his winner's share of over $250,000.

In 1970, Al had about as good a year as any racer has ever had. He won his first Indianapolis 500. He also became the only person ever to win racing's Triple Crown, the three 500-mile races then on the Indy-car circuit: Indy, Ontario, and Pocono. In total, he won 10 of 18 races (which tied a record set by A.J. Foyt) and the USAC national championship.

"When it came to those long races, like the 500s, Al Sr. was going to be there," one racing expert said.

Al Unser Sr. raises his arm in victory after winning his first Indianapolis 500 on May 31, 1970.

The 1971 Indy 500 saw Unser start in third position. The first, second, and fourth cars were all McLaren M-16s, a new car designed by Bruce McLaren that featured a spoiler wing in back and two small ones in front. Unser commented before the race, "Our only hope of winning is to put pressure on these M-16s and hope they won't hold up."

Mark Donahue, in one of the M-16s, blazed out to a 30-second lead. He ran his 66th lap at 174.91 mph—six miles an hour faster than any one had previously run a lap in traffic. On the next lap his car broke down. "When I saw Donahue was out," Unser said, "my heart did an extra lurch because I knew everyone else had a chance."

Al Unser Sr. takes the checkered flag in his Johnny Lightning Special to win the 55th running of the Indy 500 in 1971. He won with an average speed of 157.735 miles per hour.

The only other trouble Unser had came in the 113th lap when David Hobbs and Rick Muther got tangled up on the back stretch. "I came out of the fourth turn and saw them banging around, debris flying. I started to lock up my brakes. Trouble was, I couldn't see any place to go, so I decided to try the low route. If one of those cars had come sliding down across the track, I would have been history."

Al Unser became history anyway. He was the fourth person ever to win back-to-back Indy 500s.

In 1972, Unser had to settle for second behind Mark Donahue at the Indianapolis 500. Jerry Grant originally finished in front of Unser, but he was penalized 10 places for taking gas from Bobby's pit when his own tanks ran dry. If Unser seemed lucky to be awarded second place, that luck soon ran out. He didn't win another race all year. He didn't win again at the Indianapolis 500 until 1978, when he beat Tom Sneva.

Each year, between March and October, Indy cars compete in one of two racing series all over the world. The races are sanctioned by one of two organizations: the Indy Racing League (IRL) and the Champ Car World Series (CCWS). The organizations are to Indy-car racing what the National Football League (NFL) is to pro football. The IRL sets the Indy-car racing rules.

Before 1996, there was just one league, called Championship Auto Racing Teams (CART). In 1985, Al Sr. won the CART/PPG (Pittsburgh Plate Glass) Cup championship by one point, 151 to 150, over Al Jr. with 11 top-10 finishes in 14 races. It was the closest championship battle in Indy-car history and the first and only time a father and son finished first and second in the championship point standings. (Indy-car drivers are awarded points for each race: 20 for first place and 16 for second. The fastest qualifier—the driver with the fastest average speed in four laps driven before the race—gets a point, and so does the driver who led for the most laps in the race. The season's champion gets over $1 million.)

Al Sr. had driven against his son as hard as he could that year. "It's the same way I treated my brother Bobby when we were racing together," Al Sr. said. "But that feeling was a lot easier to handle than this one."

As Memorial Day of 1987 approached, Al found himself without a good ride for the Indy 500, despite his distinguished record as a driver.

Al Unser Jr. shows Al Sr. his T-shirt and gets a playful jab in return. The father–son racing rivals battled each other for the CART national championship in 1985. Al Sr. won by one point; Al Jr. came in second.

"I had never been at Indianapolis without a ride," Al said in 1987. "It was a very lonely, empty feeling." He finally found one with Roger Penske's team when Danny Ongais crashed in the first week of practice. Penske provided a left-over Ford March that he had been displaying at auto shows. Al was almost completely unfamiliar with the car, but he managed to qualify for the 20th position.

The 1987 Indy 500 started off poorly for Al. In the first turn of the race, a driver spun into the wall, barely missing him. Then Al stalled out when leaving the first pit stop, an unusual mistake for him. "Come on, Al! Pay attention to what you're supposed to be doing!" he told himself.

Slowly but surely moving forward, Al was driving in the top 10 by Lap 50 and in the top five by Lap 60. Finally he was third, behind Mario Andretti and Roberto Guerrero. "There was no way I could run with Mario," Al said—until Mario's engine quit 60 miles from the finish.

Guerrero took the lead, but he was having problems too. An overheated clutch kept slipping. He and Al fought to reach the checkered flag. When the flag flashed down, Al had won his fourth Indy 500 by 4.5 seconds.

"The Speedway has been good to me, you know," Al commented. In 1991 he was inducted into the International Motorsports Hall of Fame of America.

DID YOU KNOW?

NASCAR legend Jeff Gordon never raced in the Indy 500, which Al Sr. won four times.

But Gordon, who grew up near Indianapolis, always treasured coming to the Brickyard. In 2004, he joined Al Unser Sr., A.J. Foyt, and Rick Mears as the only drivers to win four times at Indianapolis Motor Speedway. Of course, all four of Gordon's victories were in the Brickyard 400, a NASCAR race.

Even so, Gordon got his four victories in the shortest time of any driver. Mears got his four wins in 14 tries, followed by Foyt (20 tries) and Al Sr. (22 tries). It took Gordon 11 races at the Brickyard to win four times.

Like his boyhood idols, Gordon got to kiss the bricks.

In 1994, Al failed to drive fast enough in practice laps to qualify for the Indy 500. "It takes 100 percent to race one of these cars," Al Sr. said. "I finally realized I wasn't producing like I should. I can't tell the mechanics what the car's doing, and I should be able to. If the car was perfect, maybe I could go out there and run." Al announced his retirement a few days before the race.

Ironically, after he retired, the quietest Unser found more time to play the race-car sponsorship game. When a company invests big money in a racing team, the drivers are often expected to show up at company meetings, shake hands with corporate vice presidents, make personal appearances—whatever will help company sales. Before, Al had always preferred driving, spending time at the family lodge in Chama, New Mexico (Al has been married twice and also has a daughter, Mary Linda), and avoiding idle conversation.

Sponsors are critical in the expensive sport of Indy-car racing. Each car costs about $600,000, and a driver needs two cars in case one breaks down. The driver and race team have to be paid. A huge tractor-trailer hauls the cars and serves as an on-site machine shop. A year of Indy-car racing easily runs into millions of dollars.

Five or 10 years ago, driving ability used to be all that mattered in racing. But in the high-technology age, racing has gotten so expensive that no one can afford to race without sponsors.

Al Sr. announced his retirement from racing just days short of his 55th birthday. If he had raced at Indy, it would have been his 28th appearance.

But as a birthday present for him, Al Jr. won the 1994 Indianapolis 500.

4

AL JR.: NAPOLEON AT THE RACETRACK

"I've always loved racing," said Al Unser, Jr. (Al Jr.). "I worked in a machine shop when I was 15 to get the money to buy my car. I never wanted to pursue anything else. I thought that if I could be halfway successful with racing, then I'd stay with it."

During the 1990s, Al Jr. was considered the top driver on the Indy-car circuit and one of the top five drivers in the world.

He began riding dirt bikes at the age of 6. The next year, his father gave him a minibike, and when he was 9, Al Jr. started driving go-karts. "My dad would tell me if I made a mistake and how to correct it," Al Jr. said. "But he never raised his voice at me about my driving."

"I wanted him to race," Al Sr. said. "When we started in go-karts, it was me pushing it. I think I got more of a charge out of it than he did. We used to go out every weekend and run the karts. That's how he got started. Everybody kept saying, 'He's going to be three times better than you.' And I always used to say that I hoped he was, but one step at a time. Al always progressed very rapidly, and he was good at racing."

Al Unser Jr. acknowledges fans and celebrates his victory at the 2000 Vegas Indy 300 at the Las Vegas Speedway in Las Vegas, Nevada.

Al Jr. entered his first professional race in the World of Outlaws series when he was 16. He drove a sprint car: a small, dirt-track racer. "Racing sprint cars on the dirt taught me to hustle the race car and run wheel to wheel," he said. "The World of Outlaws series was a good place to learn because it was very aggressive racing." After he finished high school, Al Jr. started racing on dirt tracks full time.

"I just couldn't believe that an 18-year-old could do what he could," Al Sr. said about his son's performance in sprint cars.

Al Jr.'s talent as a driver was clear from an early age. But racing wasn't something he had to do as a living. Financial necessity wouldn't drive him the way it had his father and uncle. "One thing I had trouble with him doing is making sure he focused in," Al Sr. remarked.

"Probably Al Jr. had everything he ever wanted," said a friend of his. "At some point, though, he had to buckle down and say, 'Okay, I want to be a race-car driver and I'm going to work hard to do that.' And he did."

After sprint cars, Al Jr. moved up to Super Vees—race cars with Volkswagen engines. (Racing Super Vees used to be like playing triple-A baseball in that these cars were the last stop before Indy cars or the pros.)

When he was 19, the Sports Car Club of America (SCCA) named Al Jr. Rookie of the Year. In 1983, he won at Pike's Peak, setting a record and ensuring that the family legend of winning there would continue.

At age 21, Al Jr. was a rookie driver in the Indy 500 race. "For the first time I had butterflies in my stomach at a race-track," he said.

Al Jr. knew about his father's legendary wins at the Indy 500 mostly through hearsay. He was too young to be at Indianapolis for his father's first two wins there, in 1970 and 1971, and he missed the third in 1978 when his parents left him at home in Albuquerque after catching him ditching school.

"This is not a magical place," Al Sr. reassured him. "It's just another racetrack, and if you treat it like that, you'll be all right." Al Jr. became the youngest driver to pass the 200-mile-per-hour barrier at Indy, and he placed 10th in that race. In 1984, he won his first Indy-car victory, at Portland International Raceway, on Father's Day.

Al Unser Jr. (right) gets doused by his father, Al Unser Sr., after winning the Budweiser Cleveland Grand Prix in 1985. Al Sr. finished third.

By 1986, he was the youngest International Race of Champions (IROC) winner, taking three of four races in the series. In IROC races, all drivers use identical cars, so that only the drivers' skill is tested.

In 1990, Unser won six CART races, tying the record for races won in a single season with Uncle Bobby (1979), Rick Mears (1981), Mario Andretti (1984), and Bobby Rahal (1986).

By winning four consecutive Indy-car races at Toronto, Michigan, Denver, and Vancouver in 1990, Al Jr. established a CART record for victories in succession (four). He became the first second-generation Indy-car champion in history, with 210 points, and the first Indy-car driver to break the 200-point record.

"Winning the championship means we accomplished the goal we set at the beginning of the season," said Al Jr. "It means all the hard work and all the dedication, desire, and sacrifice that it takes to win the title is worth it."

Unser's intensity about and commitment to racing were well known. It was said that if he had nothing to do but drive a race car, he would have been behind the wheel 365 days a year.

Because racing is a total commitment of most of a person's life, Al Jr. has had an advantage from belonging to a racing family. But not all the family reinforcement is positive. "I've heard Al say that after he won the 1990 Indy-car series points championship, his dad and uncle told him, 'You ain't nothin' until you've won Indy,'" said Paul Tracy, the third driver on the 1994 Penske Indy 500 team. "And then he won Indy [in the 1990s], and they said, 'You still aren't much—we've won it seven times.' That's a lot to live up to."

Al's racing style was said to be a combination of his uncle's and his father's styles. Bobby usually jumped out front in a race and stayed there. Al Sr. usually waited around for 100 or 120 laps before he made his move.

"Uncle Bobby was the kind of driver who could take a car that wasn't working very well and drive it a little out of control. He could do that and make the car go faster than it should," said Al Jr. "I'm like Dad. If it doesn't come, it doesn't come. The car's got to be right."

Al Unser Jr. won six races in 1988, two races in 1989, and six races and the season championship in 1990. But in 1991, 1992, and 1993 he won only one race in each year. According to one of his teammates, Al wanted a change.

Unser joined Team Penske at the end of 1993. He would race for Penske in the 1994 racing season, including at the Indianapolis 500.

At the 1994 Indy 500, Al Jr. had a score to settle with teammate Emerson Fittipaldi. Sitting in the front yard of Al Jr.'s home, in Albuquerque, is a section of the wall from the Indianapolis Motor Speedway. The wall is a piece of the old turn three, the spot Al Jr. slammed into on the 198th lap of the 1989 Indy 500. Al Jr., leading at the time, touched wheels with Fittipaldi and was knocked out of the race on the next-to-last lap.

"Fittipaldi used Al Jr. as a wall," a friend commented. Fittipaldi sped on to win the race. Unfortunately the 1994 Indy was turning out to be Fittipaldi's race, too. Only 15 laps remained, and Fittipaldi had at least a 40-second lead, almost a full lap. The Brazilian driver shot his No. 2 red-and-white Penske-Mercedes into Lap 185 of the track.

Just ahead of Emerson Fittipaldi, in car No. 31, was Al Jr. But Unser only looked like he was in the lead since he was almost a full lap down. Fittipaldi had won the previous year's Indy 500 in addition to the 1989 race, and he had run the fastest lap of this day's race: 220.680 miles per hour on Lap 121.

"If we can lead this race without abusing the car, we'll do that," Al Jr. remarked about his team before the race. "If we can't, we'll sit back and see what happens."

But from the beginning, Fittipaldi and Unser had easily outpaced the other cars with their new Penske-Mercedes engines. By the 13th lap, Unser and Fittipaldi were lapping other cars. By the 38th lap, only 16 cars were running on the lead lap, and by the 57th lap only eight cars were. On the 70th lap, Fittipaldi, Unser, and rookie Jacques Villeneuve had the lead lap to themselves. By Lap 74, only the two Penske drivers had the lead lap. Paul Tracy, the third member of the Penske team, was out on Lap 29 with engine trouble and would finish 23rd.

Al Unser Jr. leads teammate Emerson Fittipaldi into the first turn of the 78th running of the Indianapolis 500, May 1994.

Fittipaldi led for 145 laps of the race and Unser for 48, putting the team in the lead for 193 of the 200 laps total. Villeneuve, who would take second place with his Ford-Cosworth (an engine made in England by Cosworth for Ford), said, "I couldn't catch the Penskes."

Though the Penske cars had more horsepower—about 800, or as much as 200 horsepower more than the rest of the field—and handled better than the other cars, the race wasn't theirs for the taking. Al Jr. had almost crashed during a rainy practice session before the race. "That scared me," he said. "When I went out to qualify, I had to build my confidence back up. If you've ever looked down a double-barreled shotgun, that was close to what it felt like."

Unser did get his car working well in the actual race. He had won the pole, or best starting position, with a qualifying speed of 228.011 miles per hour. But he was under no illusions that he had the race in the bag. "They say that on the last lap, you can hear every nut and bolt in your car. I was just wishing my Mercedes engine would keep running," he said.

The Andretti legend of horrors at Indianapolis continued when on Lap 23 a $50 fuel pressure relief valve broke in Mario Andretti's car, putting him out of the race. Michael Andretti was penalized for passing a car while the track was under a yellow caution flag and took sixth.

Once the Mercedes cars had established their dominance in the 1994 Indy 500, another kind of race began. Though Fittipaldi and Unser were teammates, driving for the same sponsors and owner, they fought for the lead against each other.

"On race day, Emerson is another car out there for me to pass to win the race," Unser said. "Once the green flag drops, he becomes the enemy."

On Lap 185, Fittipaldi passed Unser in Turn 1. Al Jr. regained the lead on the backstretch. "Emmo was the strongest player," Unser said. "There were times when I went through a corner, my elbows were going crazy. I was getting sideways. I kept putting front wing [to produce downforce and improve traction] onto the car. Then with the last set of tires, the stagger went away."

Unser's radio had broken, so he couldn't communicate with his pit crew. When he drove by the pit, they had to wave signs to tell him when he needed to stop for fuel and new tires. But with the radio out, no one could talk to him about racing strategy.

Suddenly Fittipaldi attempted to pass Unser once more. Though it looked like an unnecessary move, Fittipaldi really had to pass or risk losing the race.

Al Jr. didn't need to make any more pit stops in the race, but Fittipaldi had to make one. Pit stops take about 15 seconds if accidents don't happen, such as a crew member getting tangled up in a fuel line. The driver can make a mistake at a pit stop. Even Unser, a master at pitting, had stalled out on one pit stop in the race, losing precious seconds. Race-car engines are prone to stalling coming out of the pit; they function better at higher speeds because the turbocharger isn't making full power when they're idling or running slow.

But the real problem Fittipaldi faced with his last pit stop was that while he was pitting, Al Jr. would get farther out in front of him. Though Al would still be most of a lap down, a wild card would remain in the race: yellow caution flags.

When danger exists on the track—for example, from a wreck or stalled car—the yellow caution flag is waved and the drivers must slow down and are not allowed to pass one another. But they are allowed to close the distance to the car ahead of them.

If there had been a yellow at the end of the 1994 Indy 500, after Fittipaldi had pitted for the last time, Al Jr. could have come all the way around the track until his car's nose was right under Fittipaldi's tailpipe.

So Fittipaldi had a choice: Don't pass Al Jr. and hope there isn't a caution, or if there is, bet you can win a close race with Al right behind you. A second choice was to pass him. Fittipaldi went for the pass.

"You're not always thinking straight at the speeds those guys are going," said Owen Snyder. The long race might have taken its toll, too. (At the time of Fittipaldi's pass, the drivers had been racing for over three hours, and they had sweated off six to eight pounds.)

As Fittipaldi tried to pass, his car got caught in the turbulent air behind Unser's car. "The turbulence just washes out the front end when you get behind someone," Unser explained. "When he passed me, I had to get on the brakes hard and I barely made it. We came up on a lot of traffic and I was able to get back by him. He just went out too far and the old vacuum cleaner got him."

"I had everything under control," Fittipaldi said regretfully. "Then going into turn four, I hit the apron. I just lost the back end. I was just about hitting the apron on every corner."

His car spun up across the track in turn four, smacked into the outer wall, and skidded in a fiery swirl down the main straightaway along the inner wall. The moment was almost an exact replay in reverse of Unser's crash in the 1992 Indy.

"I saw him hit the fence in my mirror," said Al Jr. "I felt bad for him for about a second." But he understood why Fittipaldi had attempted to pass. "Here at Indianapolis, when you see a heavy hitter in front of you, you're going to do everything you can to put him a lap down. That would've put the final nail in my coffin."

Al Jr. finished the 1994 race at a leisurely speed under a yellow caution flag after Stan Fox hit the wall on Lap 196 and the debris was cleared.

And then Unser had won his second Indianapolis 500, at an average speed of 160.872 miles per hour, 15 miles per hour below the record average speed for the race. (Crashes and yellow caution flags had brought down the average speed.) The grueling race had lasted 3 hours, 6 minutes, and 29 seconds.

Unser beat his average speed of 134.477 miles per hour in his 1992 Indy 500 win and took home $1,373,813.

Al Jr. had just added another Indy 500 trophy to the eight the Unser racing family had won in the 28 years since Al Jr.'s uncle Bobby won the Indy 500 in 1968.

After the race, Al Jr. chugged the traditional bottle of milk given to the winner at the track. Then he and his father took a victory lap together in a pace car, the very car that Al Sr. had won his last Indy 500 with in 1987, to celebrate Al Sr.'s retirement and 55th birthday. Al Jr. presented his victory as a birthday present to his father.

"This was neat. Real neat. I couldn't be happier and more emotional," Al Sr. said later, leaning against his motor home parked near the track.

But the victory scene wasn't entirely pleasant. Before, during, and after the race, squawks of unfair play were heard about the Penske cars from other racing teams.

The wondrous Penske-Mercedes engines had been designed and built in England in just over six months. They were push-rod, similar to an ordinary car engine, instead of the overhead-cam the other Indy cars used. A loophole in the racing rules allowed push-rod engines about 20 percent more horsepower than the usual overhead-cam type of race-car engine. The Mercedes engines had 55 inches of boost because of their push-rod design, while the rest of the field was allowed only 45 inches. The increased boost gave the Penske cars their horsepower advantage over the other cars in the Indy 500.

"They'll lose only if they screw up," said rival owner Derrick Walker of the Penske drivers before the race.

"They weren't even letting the cars all the way out," remarked Owen Snyder, team manager of Galles International

Al Unser Jr. drives the Penske car to victory in the 1994 Indy Car Long Beach Grand Prix in 1994. In 1995, the rules were changed regarding engine specifications and the Penske-Mercedes engine had to be totally redesigned.

Racing, which also ran a team against the Penske cars. "They were saving them."

Unser deserved credit for excellent, experienced driving in the race. He was no raw rookie at Indianapolis—he had won 20 races and almost $12 million in 13 seasons on the Indy-car circuit before the 1994 Indy.

But no one disagreed that the Penske cars were the best at the race. Some said that only Roger Penske, with his finances and his determination to have an edge, could have successfully pulled off the Penske miracle at Indianapolis. "Roger Penske gets things done," Al Sr. remarked.

"The Penske engine was just fine-tuning," said Bobby Unser. "Buick was building that same engine for probably 12 years without the success that Penske had; he just spent more money and made his a little better. Penske built the engine to the edge of the rules. Basically, real innovation isn't happening anymore in race-car design."

"We'll catch the Penske team," said Owen Snyder. "Galles had 17 wins with Al Jr. from 1988 through 1993 against Penske's big bucks. Hard work does pay off."

In June 1994, the USAC changed the rules of racing so that the Penske cars couldn't have more than 52 inches of boost. Then in mid-August they limited the boost to 48 inches.

"This was politically motivated—no engineering data were collected before the change was made," Penske said angrily of the last restriction. In effect the 1994 Penske engines, with their 55 inches of boost, had to be totally redesigned for 1995. By 1996 the rule will be that all Indy cars have the same engine: a four-cam turbocharged racing engine with a 2.2-liter capacity. This is the same design the Ford-Cosworth and other engines currently running in Indy cars now have but half a liter smaller.

In the meantime, more Penske-Unser victories followed in 1994 in Milwaukee, Portland, Cleveland, and Lexington, Ohio, all races in the Indy-car series. Al Jr. won those races after Indianapolis with an ordinary Ilmor/D engine—not the supercharged Penske-Mercedes V-8. He won the 1994 Indy-car series championship.

In 1995, Al Jr. had another successful year, winning four races and finishing second in the season standings. The following year, when CART and the IRL began breaking up, Al Jr. finished fourth. But then, things started to slip. In the 1997 CART standings, Al Jr. finished 13th. The next year, he was 11th, then 21st.

Things started going terribly for Al Jr. Not only was he fired from the Penske team, but he was going through a messy divorce, which was finalized in late 1999. He soon left CART for the IRL, which meant he could race in the Indy 500 once again.

But Al Jr.'s on-the-track career couldn't make up for his off-the-track problems. In 2002, he checked himself into an alcohol rehabilitation center. Then, in late 2003, Al Jr. was seriously injured in an all-terrain vehicle accident near his

Did you know?

Al Unser Jr. once won six races in a single season, a record he shares with Bobby Rahal, among others.

Rahal picked up a big win of another kind in 2004. Teaming with late night talk show host David Letterman, the new Rahal Letterman Racing organization won the Indianapolis 500 behind the racing of driver Buddy Rice.

Letterman is from Indiana, so his passion for Indy car racing was instilled as a youngster. He joined Team Rahal in the mid-1990s as a minority partner. In 2002, he received a big thrill when he became a co-owner of the team and entered a car in the Indy 500.

"Having grown up in Indianapolis and been in love with racing and its heroes for as long as I can remember, it's literally a dream come true for me to become this much a part of a sport that has meant so much to me," Letterman said on the team's website, *http://irl.rahal. com/main.php.*

home in New Mexico. He broke his pelvis in several places, and his recovery was painful and lengthy.

In 2004, Al Jr. joined a new race team, Patrick Racing. He ran several races in 2004, but after a disappointing finish in the summer race at Richmond, Al Jr. announced his retirement.

"You just know when it's time," he told the Associated Press. "I never had set a date, but you have to have a passion for it. I'm no longer willing to maintain that level of sacrifice or desire."[1]

Al Jr.'s retirement ended a career which saw 34 total wins in the CART and IRL series. He won two CART championships and two Indy 500s.

"I feel I upheld the Unser name quite well," he said.[2]

5

"JUST AL" AND THE UNSER LEGACY

When Al Jr. retired in the summer of 2004, racing fans wondered what would happen to the famous Unser name. But that's where Alfred Richard Unser comes in.

The next Unser has told reporters he wants to be called "Just Al." In 2005, Just Al is only 22 years old and starting on what he hopes will be a long and successful racing career.

Just Al is the son of Al Jr., the grandson of Al Sr., and the great nephew of Bobby. If your name is anything like "Al Unser" and you don't drive a race car, people would wonder what went wrong.

That's what Just Al's mother, Shelley, told the *Detroit Free Press* in July 2004.

"My biggest hope was for him to get an opportunity to try everything, so he wouldn't have to wonder 'What if?' as an Unser," she said.[3]

According to the *Free Press*, Just Al was well on his way to a racing career, whizzing around in go-karts like many other drivers who start young. But at age 12, he suddenly quit.

But when he got his driver's permit at age 15, the *Free Press* reported, Just Al was ready to try racing again. He told the newspaper that it was "in the genes."

Al Unser Jr. announced his retirement from racing in 2004 at the Indianapolis Motor Speedway. With over 30 wins, including two CART championships and two Indy 500s, Al Jr. felt he upheld the Unser name.

If Just Al continues with his racing career, he'll represent the fourth generation of Unser drivers. He finished 2004 in the Infiniti Pro series, but he has also raced in the Toyota Atlantic series, the Barber Dodge series and the Skip Barber Western series, where he was Rookie of the Year in 2002.

Just Al even has a website called *www.justalracing.com.* The motto on the home page reads, "Yes, Just Al. No, not 'the third.' And not the other ones either. Just Al. Just Al Unser. And Just Al Unser Racing. Period."[4]

Infinity Pro Series driver "Just Al" Unser (right) talks with his grandfather, Al Unser Sr., after a practice session at the Indianapolis Motor Speedway in 2005.

Just Al's website reveals many different interests: he's trained as a professional movie stuntman, he's qualified to work with killer whales and dolphins, he's an "expert" snowmobiler, and he's competed in equestrian events.

Those activities all sound risky, but one of Just Al's scariest moments was a wreck in August 2002. Just Al was racing in the Skip Barber Dodge series when he crashed, flipping and rolling over and over.

The *Vancouver Sun* reported that when Just Al was loaded into the ambulance, the paramedic asked for the patient's name, causing the following exchange:

"Al Unser," Just Al said.

"Son, that's not funny," the paramedic replied.

"No sir," Just Al said. "My name is Al Unser."[5]

Just Al recovered, but he realizes he's lucky. His sister, Cody, is paralyzed from the chest down with a rare disease

DID YOU KNOW?

Cody Unser was a normal sixth grader or as normal as you can get being part of a famous racing family.

During basketball practice in 1999, Cody began to feel "excessively tired, had difficulty catching her breath, developed a pounding headache, and her legs felt heavy, numb, and tingly."*

The next day, she was paralyzed from the chest down due to a spinal cord inflammation called Transverse Myelitis.

Today, the Cody Unser First Step Foundation helps raise awareness and money for Transverse Myelitis research.

She'll probably never drive a race car, but Cody Unser has made an impact on the world in her own way. Cody's drive to cure paralysis is more important than any race could ever be.

*"A paralyzing disease doesn't keep this Indy 500 winner's daughter from reaching for the stars," *Sports 'N Spokes*, Fly 2003, *www.cufsf.org/pdf/sns.pdf*.

called transverse myelitis. Just Al told *The Oregonian* in 2003 that he uses his sister for motivation.

"To see her inspire people the way she does, it makes you really step back and look at life," Just Al said. "It has really made me focus on what I want to do."[6]

Someday, Just Al might add to his family's nine Indianapolis 500 titles. After all, this isn't just a normal family—it's the legendary Unsers.

NOTES

Chapter 4

1. Michael Marot, "Ebbing passion hastens retirement by 'Little Al,'" *The Associated Press*, July 1, 2004.

2. Ibid.

Chapter 5

3. George Sipple, "'Just Al' content to be himself," *Detroit Free Press*, July 31, 2004.

4. The Official Website of Just Al Racing—The Race Team of Just Al Unser! *www.justalracing.com.*

5. Gary Mason, "A Chip Off the Old Block," *The Vancouver Sun*, July 23, 2003.

6. Dave Charbonneau, "Latest Unser Creates Own Identity," *The Oregonian*, July 22, 2003.

CHRONOLOGY

Bobby Unser

1934 Born on February 20 in Colorado Springs, Colorado.

1949 Starts racing stock cars in New Mexico.

1950–1951 Wins Southwest Modified Stock Car Championship both years.

1952 Begins racing midget and sprint cars; wins three races.

1953–1955 Serves in U.S. Air Force in Albuquerque, New Mexico, and races midget and sprint cars there and at Pike's Peak Hill climb.

1956 Wins championship car division at the Pike's Peak Hill climb, first win of what will eventually be a record 13 Pike's Peak titles.

1963 Runs first Indy 500. An accident early in the race forces him out of the event.

1967 Wins first Indy-1 car race at Mosportin in Ontario, Canada. Sets a new track record; first win of 35 career IndyCar Series victories (fourth all-time).

1968 Wins first Indy 500 at record speed; first driver to run over 170 miles per hour at an IndyCar Series track. Wins United States Auto Club (USAC) National Driving championship.

1970 Places second to Al Sr. in USAC standings.

1972 Sets new qualifying mark at Indianapolis of 195.940 miles per hour; biggest leap in speed record in the history of the race. Fastest qualifier in eight of nine races run for the year, and led all nine races for a total of 520 laps. First driver to qualify at an average speed of over 200 mph (201.374).

1974 Captures second USAC National Driving Championship and named Martini & Rossi Driver of the Year. Wins first California 500.

1975 Wins second Indy 500 and International Race of Champions (IROC) title.

1979 Wins six races in Championship Auto Racing Teams (CART) IndyCar Series.

1980 Wins fourth California 500 (1974, 1976, 1979, 1980); only driver ever to win race four times.

1981 Wins third Indy 500.

1983 As car owner-team manager, wins Pike's Peak Hill climb with Al Jr. driving.

1986 Wins Pike's Peak Hill climb as driver in Audi Sport Quattro SL after 12-year absence from race.

1987 Begins work as commentator for ABC Sports Television.

1993 Wins inaugural Jaguar/Fastmasters Championship at Indianapolis Raceway Park. Sets new land speed record of 223.709 at the Bonneville Salt Flats with a gas-powered modified roadster.

2004 Turns 70 years old and publishes business-related book entitled *Winners are Driven: A Champion's Guide to Success in Business and Life.*

Al Unser Sr.

1939 Born on May 29 in Albuquerque, New Mexico.

1957 First race in modified roadster in Albuquerque.

1960 First Pike's Peak Hill climb comes in second to brother Bobby.

1964 Wins first Pike's Peak Hill climb, setting new course record and breaking Bobby's six-race winning streak.

1965 Wins second Pike's Peak Hill climb. Drives in first Indy 500, finishing ninth.

1967 Comes in second at Indy 500 to A.J. Foyt. Named Rookie of the Year in USAC stock cars.

1969 Breaks leg in a motorcycle crash during his birthday party in Gasoline Alley the night before the Indy 500 and misses race.

1970 Wins 10 of 18 races on USAC championship trial, including the Indy 500. Named Martini & Rossi Driver of the Year and USAC national champion.

1971 Fourth (and last) driver to win two consecutive Indy 500s.

1973 Wins USAC's dirt championship and Texas 200.

1974 Finishes 0.5 seconds behind Bobby in the Ontario and 500 and the California 500.

1976 Drives first car with a Cosworth Ford engine ever to win an IndyCar Series race, the Pocono 500.

1977 Wins first California 500; champion of the IROC series.

1978 First to win the Triple Crown series of 500s: Indy, Pocono, and Ontario. Wins IROC series for second straight year.

1983 Wins the Cleveland 500 and the CART/PPG Cup title with 10 top-5 finishes in 13 races.

1985 Co-drives with A.J. Foyt and others to win the Daytona 24-hour race. Wins CART/PPG Cup championship by one point over Al Jr. with 11 top-10 finishes in 14 races. Leads Triple Crown drivers in points.

1987 Wins fourth Indy 500, subbing for an injured driver, after starting 20th. Ties all-time record of 613 laps led at Indy.

1991 Inducted into Motorsports Hall of Fame of America.

1994 Retires from racing at Indianapolis 500, Memorial Day weekend, on his 55th birthday.

1996 Becomes consultant and coach for the newly formed Indy Racing League (IRL).

Al Unser Jr.

1962 Born on April 19 in Albuquerque, New Mexico.

1979–1980 Competes in World of Outlaws series. Meets future wife, Shelley, at Manzanita Speedway in Phoenix in 1980.

1981 Wins Sports Car Club of America (SCCA) Super Vee title and Rookie of the Year honors.

1982 Places fifth in IndyCar Series debut in the California 500 at Riverside International Raceway.

1983 Youngest driver to pass the 200-mile-per-hour barrier at the Indianapolis Motor Speedway. First Pike's Peak Hill climb win, setting record as youngest winner.

1984 Wins first IndyCar Series race at Portland International Raceway on Father's Day.

1985 Edged out for the CART/PPG championship by Al Sr. by a single point, 151–150.

1986 Finishes more races (14), completes more miles (3,782) and more laps (2,188) than any other driver en route to a fourth-place finish in the CART/PPG championship point standings. At age 24, youngest IROC driver in the series history.

1987 Wins second consecutive Daytona 24-hour race.

1988 Joins Galles International Racing in Albuquerque. Records four IndyCar Series victories. Wins second IROC title with victory at Watkins Glen.

1990 Wins first CART/PPG championship, becoming first-ever second-generation IndyCar Series champion. Ties record for races won in single season (six). Wins four consecutive races, establishing a CART record. Earns first IndyCar oval-track win at Milwaukee and first 500-mile win at Michigan in the fastest 500-mile auto race in history (average speed, 189.727 miles per hour).

1992 Wins first Indy 500 in closest race (by six feet) in Indy 500 history. With Al Sr.'s victories, first time a father and son have won the race.

1994 Joins Penske racing team. Wins second Indy 500. More victories follow in the Toyota Grand Prix in Long Beach, California, as well as IndyCar Series races in Milwaukee, Portland, and Cleveland; CART/PPG series point leader.

1995 Earns four consecutive podium finishes with wins at Mid-Ohio and Long Beach.

1996 Becomes the driver with the most wins in the PPG IndyCar World Series history with 31 victories. His 22 victories in the 1990s are more than any other driver in the decade.

1998 Leads All-time CART leaders in winnings, with more than $18 million in his career.

1999 Joins Indy Racing League, coached by father Al Sr.

2004 Retires from auto racing.

STATISTICS

Unser Wins at the Indianapolis 500

	Year	Starting Position	Average speed (mph)
Bobby Unser	1968	3	152.882
	1975	3	149.213
	1981	1	139.084
Al Unser Sr.	1970	1	155.749
	1971	5	157.735
	1978	5	161.363
	1987	20	162.175
Al Unser Jr.	1992	12	134.477
	1994	1	160.872

FURTHER READING

Arute, Jack, and Jenna Fryer. *Jack Arute's Tales from the Indy 500*. Champaign, IL: Sports Publishing, 2004.

Bentley, Ross. *Speed Secrets: Professional Race Driving Techniques*. Osceola, WI: Motorbooks International, 1998.

Doeden, Matt. *NASCAR's Wildest Wrecks*. Kentwood, LA: Edge Books, 2005.

Indianapolis Motor Speedway. *2000 Indy Review, Vol. 10*. Osceola, WI: Motorbooks International, 2001.

Kirby, Gordon. *Unser: An American Family Portrait*. New York, NY: Anion Press, 1988.

Pimm, Nancy Roe. *Indy 500: The Inside Track*. Plain City, OH: Darby Creek Publishing, 2004.

Reed, Terry. *Indy: The Race and Ritual of the Indianapolis 500*. Dulles, VA: Potomac Books, 2005.

Richards, Jon. *Fantastic Cutaway: Speed*. New York, NY: Copper Beech, 1997.

Rubel, David. *How to Drive an Indy Race Car*. Emeryville, CA: Avalon Travel Publishing, 1992.

Stewart, Mark. *Auto Racing: A History of Cars and Fearless Drivers*. London, UK: Franklin Watts, 1999.

Sullivan, George. *Racing Indy Cars*. New York, NY:
    Dutton, 1992.

Weber, Bruce. *The Indianapolis 500*. Mankato, MN:
    Creative Education, 1990.

Wicker, Ned. *Indy Car C-H-A-M-P-I-O-N: A Season with
    Target/Chip Ganassi Racing*. Osceola, WI: Motorbooks
    International, 1997.

BIBLIOGRAPHY

"A paralyzing disease doesn't keep this Indy 500 winner's daughter from reaching for the stars." *Sports 'N Spokes*, July 2003. *www.cufsf.org/pdf/sns.pdf.*

Charbonneau, Dave. "Latest Unser Creates Own Identity." *The Oregonian*, 22 July 2003.

Marot, Michael. "Ebbing passion hastens retirement by 'Little Al.'" *The Associated Press*, July 1, 2004.

Mason, Gary. "A Chip Off the Old Block." *The Vancouver Sun*, 23 July 2003.

Sipple, George. "'Just Al' content to be himself." *Detroit Free Press*, 31 July 2004.

The Associated Press. "Unser Jr. calls it a career." 30 June 2004.

The Official Website of Just Al Racing—The Race Team of Just Al Unser! *www.justalracing.com.*

Unser, Al III. Web posting on *www.justalracing.com.*

ADDRESSES

Indianapolis Motor Speedway
4790 W. 16th St.
Indianapolis, IN 46222

The Cody Unser First Step Foundation
P.O. Box 56696
Albuquerque, NM 87187

The Unser Children's Discovery Center
    and Racing Museum
7625 Central Avenue NW
Albuquerque, NM 87121

INTERNET SITES

www.indy500.com

> *The official site of the Indianapolis 500 is a comprehensive look back at the history of the race, as well as a glance toward the future. There are tons of facts and interesting tidbits to learn about the Indy 500.*

www.justalracing.com

> *Keep track of the latest Unser's racing activities. Just Al Racing's website has the latest schedules and news for "Just Al" or Al Unser III.*

www.theunsers.com

> *Follow the progress of the Unser Children's Discovery Center and Racing Museum, being built in Albuquerque, New Mexico.*

www.codysfirststep.org

> *Learn about Cody Unser's disease and what you can do to help her and others stricken by Transverse Myelitis.*

Photo Credits:

©AP/Wide World Photos: 7, 9, 11, 33, 39, 44, 54, 55; ©Bettmann/CORBIS: 16, 18, 21, 23, 29, 32, 35, 41; ©Time Life Pictures/Getty Images: 13; ©Getty Images: Cover, 49.

INDEX

ABOUT THE AUTHORS

Karen Bentley worked for Scientific American, Inc., and Random House–Knopf Children's Books in New York and has written three romances for young adults. She lives in Albuquerque, New Mexico, home of the famous Unsers.

Jeff Gluck covers NASCAR, high school sports and the Atlantic Coast Conference for the *Rocky Mount Telegram* in North Carolina. A University of Delaware graduate, Gluck has also lived in California, Minnesota, and Colorado, visiting a total of 45 states along the way. Gluck has covered the Super Bowl, the Daytona 500, a Duke-North Carolina men's college basketball game, and has attended three NCAA Final Fours.

Local coverage includes every high school sport from football to swimming, as well as the Double-A Carolina Mudcats baseball team, and NCAA Division III N.C. Wesleyan College.

Gluck and his wife, Jaime, reside in Rocky Mount, North Carolina.